VGM Opportunities Series

OPPORTUNITIES IN **EDUCATIONAL SUPPORT CAREERS**

Mark Rowh

Foreword by
Andy Brantley
President
College and University Professional Association for Human
Resources (CUPA-HR)
Assistant Vice President for Business Administration and
Director of Human Resources, Davidson College

 **VGM Career Books**

Library of Congress Cataloging-in-Publication Data

Rowh, Mark.
  Opportunities in educational support careers / Mark Rowh ; foreword by Andy
    Brantley.
    p. cm. — (VGM opportunities series)
    ISBN 0-658-00049-7 (hardcover)
    ISBN 0-658-00050-0 (paperback)
    1. School employees — Vocational guidance. I. Title. II. Series.

  LB2831.5 .R69 2001
  371'.0023—dc21

                                                              00-68665

Cover photograph copyright © PhotoDisc

Published by VGM Career Books
A division of The McGraw-Hill Companies.
4255 West Touhy Avenue, Lincolnwood (Chicago), Illinois 60712-1975 U.S.A.
Printed in the United States of America
International Standard Book Number: 0-658-00049-7 (hardcover)
                                    0-658-00050-0 (paperback)

1   2   3   4   5   6   7   8   9   0   LB/LB   0   9   8   7   6   5   4   3   2   1

DEDICATION

This book is dedicated to all those people who have labored in the background to help provide students with a chance to improve their lives.

CONTENTS

About the Author.................................. vii

Foreword... ix

Acknowledgments xi

Introduction xiii

1. Supporting the Educational Enterprise 1

Employers of educational support personnel. Career
advantages in educational support. Flexible career prospects.
Do you have what it takes to succeed in an educational
support career? Questions to ask yourself.

2. Educational Administrators 9

Career paths in educational administration. Representative
administrative positions. One day on the job.

3. Counselors and Student Service Specialists.......... 25

Counselors and school psychologists. College and university
student affairs. Do you have what it takes to succeed in
student services? Questions to ask yourself.

4. Librarians and Media Specialists 38

Libraries of today. College library positions. School
librarians. Do you have what it takes to succeed in a library
career? Questions to ask yourself.

5. **Public Relations and Advancement Officers**..........48

Do you have what it takes to succeed in advancement and public relations? Questions to ask yourself.

6. **Administrative Support Staff and Other Support Jobs**...................................56

Clerical and administrative support workers. Institutional research. Instructional design. Human resources. Computer support. Facilities managers and staff. Transportation.

7. **Educational Preparation**..........................73

Educational administration. Counseling programs. Library and information studies. Institutional research. Teacher's aide. Certification. Planning your education. Selecting a college. Meeting college expenses.

8. **Salaries and Benefits**............................94

Potential salary levels. Fringe benefits.

9. **Professional Associations**.......................99

Benefits of participating in professional associations. Representative professional associations.

10. **Getting Started**................................113

Finding job vacancies. Developing an appropriate background. Enhancing employment potential.

Appendix A: Further Reading.......................118

Appendix B: State Education Agencies................119

Appendix C: State Higher Education Agencies..........131

Appendix D: Canadian Departments and Ministries of Education......................142

ABOUT THE AUTHOR

Mark Rowh is a professional educator who has worked for more than twenty years in administrative positions in two- and four-year colleges. He is currently Director of Institutional Advancement at New River Community College in Dublin, Virginia.

Rowh is also a widely published writer on career topics. He has contributed several other books published by VGM Career Books and is the author of *Opportunities in Fund Raising Careers, Great Jobs for Chemistry Majors, Great Jobs for Political Science Majors, Slam Dunk Cover Letters,* and a number of other books.

He holds a master's degree in English and a doctorate in education.

FOREWORD

Schools are among the most important organizations in our society. Every year, millions of students attend elementary schools, middle schools, high schools, colleges, and universities. Serving these students is the responsibility not just of teachers, but of a host of other dedicated individuals who support the educational enterprise. Their roles are truly diverse. Some perform administrative leadership or management support functions. Some provide counseling or other student services. Some of those who work in noninstructional jobs operate libraries, perform clerical functions, care for physical facilities, or fill other roles.

In *Opportunities in Educational Support Careers*, Mark Rowh points out that while the most typical educational career may be that of the teacher or educator, it is far from the only one. The educational sector is a vast enterprise, and its personnel needs are great. Teachers cannot get their work done without the involvement of many other people. From the human resources officer who assists in hiring new faculty and staff to the media specialist who assists in developing instructional materials, key players in the educational process make a wide range of important contributions.

In addition to providing an overview of various educational support roles, Rowh includes helpful information on professional organizations, educational options, salaries and benefits, and getting started in pursuing an educational career.

Of course, any career in education requires hard work, dedication, and the appropriate credentials. But it can also offer great rewards. After all, working in this field means being a part of something larger than yourself.

Can you see yourself providing leadership as a school principal or college administrator? Or working in raising funds for scholarships or other needs? Could a role as a counselor, librarian, or public relations specialist possibly be in your future? These are just a few examples of the important roles played by those working in educational support areas. Read on and you can find out more about an array of such careers. Perhaps you will find yourself pursuing one of them.

Andy Brantley, President
College and University Professional Association for Human Resources (CUPA-HR)
Assistant Vice President for Business Administration and Director of Human Resources, Davidson College

ACKNOWLEDGMENTS

The author offers grateful thanks to the following for their cooperation in providing assistance or information for this book:

American Association of School Administrators

American College Personnel Association

American School Counselor Association

Canadian Association of Principals

College and University Professional Association for Human Resources

Linda Rowh

National Association of Secondary School Principals

Radford Library

U.S. Department of Education

U.S. Department of Labor

INTRODUCTION

"Education" is one of the most important words in the English language. After all, few concepts are more fundamentally important to a modern society. Without an educated population, life would be vastly different in the United States, Canada, and elsewhere.

Of course, education is a complex process. It requires a great commitment of resources. Thousands of schools, colleges, and other organizations exist just for this purpose. Funded by government tax dollars, private support, tuition paid by students and their families—or by a combination of these resources—educational institutions provide a place where people from all kinds of backgrounds can go to learn.

At the same time, schools and colleges are much more than buildings. In a real sense, they are actually made up of people. In addition to the students who attend them, these institutions are made up of specialized employees. Teachers and other personnel perform a wide range of important services to help students acquire the knowledge they need to live, work, and fully participate in society.

Of course, teachers or professors form the heart of any educational institution. The direct role of instructing students is the central task at hand, but teachers are by no means the only employees to be found in the educational sector. To the contrary, other types of workers also perform highly important roles. Educational support personnel are an integral part of every educational institution.

Within the context of this book, "educational support" refers to all types of positions—other than those of classroom teachers or professors—that support the teaching and learning process. It includes not only the jobs that might be considered as subordinate to teachers, but also higher-level administrative positions. The overall approach is that a variety of nonteaching positions, some at the management level and others at the support staff level, provide important contributions to the overall operation of schools, colleges, and other educational organizations.

From a career perspective, this overall employment category holds great potential. Those interested in teaching may find this employment area of special interest, for it represents flexibility in career options. Many persons working in noninstructional jobs start out in teaching, and then move to administrative positions or other related roles.

At the same time, many others who are not attracted to teaching careers can find a place in the educational setting. It takes a great deal of talent, dedication, and hard work to keep any school, college, or school district running. From counselors and librarians to secretaries and business managers, other personnel perform important work in support of the main focus of helping students learn. For example, a typical college will have a chief student services officer, a chief academic officer, and several other top-level administrators, each providing leadership to a large group of professional employees and support staff.

If a school setting seems an attractive work environment and you have an interest in one of the career areas that play a role in educational institutions, you might want to consider an educational support career. Certainly, there is a need for motivated people in this area. As the population grows and as current personnel retire or otherwise leave employment, a continuing need will exist for those with the necessary talent and training to fill such roles.

CHAPTER 1

SUPPORTING THE EDUCATIONAL ENTERPRISE

Education is big business. Well over 50 million students are enrolled in the United States in schools and colleges. These include more than 46 million students in public schools, which in turn employ some 2.8 million teachers, and about 5 million students enrolled in private schools, according to the National Center for Education Statistics. In addition, Canada has more than 16,000 elementary and secondary schools and nearly 300 colleges and universities. Including public elementary and secondary schools, private schools, colleges, and universities, more than 100,000 schools serve the United States and Canada.

These various institutions, along with school district offices and other coordinating agencies, employ millions of people. Many, of course, are teachers. But many employees perform other important functions in support of the educational missions of schools.

According to the U.S. Department of Education, nearly five million staff are employed in public school systems alone in the United States. These include the following:

Type of Position	Number Employed
School district officials and administrators	49,000
School district administrative support staff	145,000
District-level instructional coordinators	37,000
Principals and assistant principals	121,000

In addition, more than 200,000 staff are employed in private elementary and secondary schools.

At the postsecondary level, more than one million persons are employed in American colleges and universities. Canada's schools, colleges, and universities also employ large numbers of administrative personnel and other support workers.

What does all this mean to you? If you're interested in a career in education, plenty of opportunities await you. This is true not just in teaching, but in a variety of support areas. From the smallest school district to the largest university, nonteaching jobs provide a host of employment opportunities.

At a large institution such as Ohio State University, scores of nonteaching positions may be open at any one time. Here is a list for a typical week's job openings, not including health care jobs in the university hospital:

Academic Program Coordinator
Accountant, University Hospitals-Financial Services
Administrative Associate 1, Maintenance
Administrative Associate 1, (Division Administrator), Surgery
Animal Caretaker
Animal Health Technician
Assistant Manager, Food Services Center for Tomorrow
Assistant Mason
Automotive Mechanic 2
Boiler Maintenance Worker
Bookbinder, Printing Services
Carpenter 1
Chaplain, University Hospitals-Pastoral Care
Computer Operator 2
Cook 1
Coordinator Academic Advising, Ohio Learning Network
Custodial Worker
Director of Event Marketing and Seating, Athletics

Director of Events, Alumni Association
Director, Strength and Conditioning, Athletics
Director, University Relations
Early Childhood Teaching Assistant
Electrician 2
Electronic Technician 2
Extension Associate, Entomology
Facility Manager, Neurobiotechnology Center
Food Service Worker
Graphic Designer, Transportation and Parking
Groundskeeper 1
Groundskeeper 2
Hazardous Waste Specialist, Environmental Health and Safety
Information Associate
Laboratory Animal Technician 2
Laboratory Demonstrator, Microbiology
Maintenance Repair Worker 1, 2, and 3
Office Assistant (several positions)
Office Associate (several positions)
Office Production Assistant
Plant Maintenance Engineer 1
Program Assistant 1, Extension County Operations
Program Assistant 2, Extension County Operations
Program Coordinator, History
Program Director, Engineering Administration
Program Manager, Reading Recovery
Program Manager, School Administration
Steam Fitter
Systems Developer/Engineer (Network Specialist/Programmer)
Systems Developer/Engineer (Reading Recovery Webmaster)
Systems Developer/Engineer (WEB Administrator, Chemistry)
Vehicle Operator 2

Of course in smaller colleges, high schools, elementary schools, and other institutions, such a large number of position openings could not be expected. But virtually every school, whatever the size or type, depends on educational support personnel to fulfill its mission.

From the organization's viewpoint, such positions are a routine part of operations. From the individual's perspective, this means that career possibilities abound for those interested in working in education.

EMPLOYERS OF EDUCATIONAL SUPPORT PERSONNEL

A variety of settings can be found in which men and women hold important positions in support of the teaching-learning process. Although obviously most employers are schools, the variety of employers or job assignments might surprise you. In school districts, the overall employer might be the school district itself, with the employee assigned to a specific school or unit.

Some places in which educational support personnel are employed or assigned include public elementary, middle, and high schools; church-supported schools; nonreligious private elementary and secondary schools; school district offices; state departments of education; regional educational service agencies; private tutoring or educational support firms; noncollegiate business/vocational or technical schools; public community and technical colleges; private junior and community colleges; private and public colleges and universities; state higher education coordinating agencies; the U.S. Department of Education; educational associations; and performing arts organizations.

This list represents most, but not all, of the potential employers of educational support personnel. With such variety, it is apparent that this career area, while more narrowly defined than some, offers diverse employment possibilities.

CAREER ADVANTAGES IN EDUCATIONAL SUPPORT

There are many advantages to be found in a career in educational support. Some of these include the opportunity to work in a school or other education-based environment, the chance to provide services of genuine importance in helping people meet their educational and career goals, and the opportunity to expand one's personal knowledge base by interacting with faculty, administrators, students, and others in the educational setting. Also important are the potential to advance in the job provided by employment in a structured organization such as a school or college; a high level of potential job mobility, since education is a universal need with thousands of schools existing to serve students; and the potential to work in a field that garners respect from others.

FLEXIBLE CAREER PROSPECTS

Another advantage of a career in an educational support area is that it may offer flexible prospects. This could mean moving into the classroom, if one possesses the necessary credentials. Or it could mean moving up within a school or other educational organization, perhaps working in executive management or other high-level positions.

At the same time, many of the skills involved in specific support areas are transferable to other career areas. For example, a school librarian may move to a city library or other public library. A counselor might go into private counseling or move to a state social services agency. An educational administrator might move into a management position in the private sector. Of course, many who work in education spend their entire careers without making such a move. In that case, it is rewarding to realize that there are literally thousands of schools, colleges, and related organizations across the United States and Canada that employ educational support personnel. For those who want to remain in the field but move to other geographic locations, the potential is also strong.

DO YOU HAVE WHAT IT TAKES TO SUCCEED IN AN EDUCATIONAL SUPPORT CAREER?

Because the educational sector includes such a wide variety of support jobs, no single set of skills or abilities applies to all positions. In general, though, the traits or skills necessary to succeed in most education-related careers include a genuine liking for people and an ability to interact effectively with others (in other words, good "people skills"), a solid sense of loyalty and commitment to the educational mission of one's employing institution, a strong sense of personal ethics, good skills in oral and written communications, and a high energy level. The ability to solve problems and work creatively to improve processes and procedures, an appreciation for the importance of teamwork, the potential to master the skills required to perform specified support functions, a value system that emphasizes broad-based goals and shared accomplishments, and a willingness to seek additional education or training to maintain or improve job-related knowledge also are necessary.

QUESTIONS TO ASK YOURSELF

No one can legitimately argue that education is unimportant. Not only is the educational sector one of the largest employers anywhere, but the work performed is vital both on individual and societal levels.

For any individual, the appropriateness of an educational support career depends not only on the overall importance of the field, but also on his or her goals, talents, and interests. In considering whether this might be an area of potential career interest, ask yourself questions such as the following: Do I believe strongly in the value of education? Do I enjoy working with people? Do I have solid communication skills? Would I mind working outside of the classroom or in the background? Do others consider me a hard worker? Am I a good team player? Would I be comfortable working in a school environment? Am I willing to obtain specialized academic preparation to prepare for a job in this field? Do I see myself working toward meeting public service needs as opposed to the profit-seeking orientation of the business world?

If your answer to most or all of these questions is "yes," you may be well suited to an education-related career. To find out more about just what is involved in various educational support jobs, take a look at the following chapters.

Chapter 2 looks at the work of educational administrators, while Chapter 3 covers the role of counselors and student service specialists.

In Chapter 4, the work of librarians and media specialists is examined, and in Chapter 5, careers for public relations and advancement officers within the educational world are considered.

Chapter 6 looks at administrative support staff and other support jobs.

Chapter 7 covers educational preparation for an educational support career, and Chapter 8 addresses salaries and benefits.

Chapter 9 includes overviews of selected professional associations, and Chapter 10 provides tips in getting started in a career in this area.

Once you have reviewed this material, perhaps you will want to take further steps in pursuing an educational support career. Who knows? A job in a school, college, or other education-related organization may await you.

CHAPTER 2

EDUCATIONAL ADMINISTRATORS

When you were in elementary school, one of the most important people in the world was the principal. Whether you viewed the principal as someone to be feared or as another friendly adult, you understood that this person was the one in charge of the school.

In every school, college, or other educational organization, someone must be in charge of day-to-day operations. In an elementary, middle, or high school this is generally the principal, who is often assisted by one or more assistant principals. In a school district, it is the superintendent. In a college or university, a president is usually the chief executive officer, with vice presidents or deans heading up major organizational units.

Although teachers provide the primary role of instruction, educational administrators also play important roles. In even the smallest school, there must be a principal, director, president, or other administrator to perform the necessary management duties to keep it operating. In larger educational organizations, whether they are schools, colleges, school districts, or other organizations, scores or even hundreds of managers may be needed at various levels. This includes not only the top-level executive positions, but a variety of upper- and middle-management jobs.

Regardless of titles, most educational administrators have responsibilities that include managing the day-to-day affairs of an educational organization, or of a unit within an educational organization; supervising teachers, nonteaching staff, and/or other managers; recruiting and hiring new personnel; evaluating the work of supervised personnel; and managing budgets. They might also represent the organization or unit to the public or other units within the same organization and plan, implement, and evaluate activities of an educational organization or a unit within such an organization.

CAREER PATHS IN EDUCATIONAL ADMINISTRATION

Typically, people don't assume management jobs as their first position in an educational career. Most educational administrators start out as teachers or staff employees and then, after gaining experience and, in many cases, acquiring additional educational credentials, they advance to administrative positions.

For example, the career path followed by one school superintendent began as a high school teacher. Then, in logical progression, she became assistant principal, principal, assistant director of curriculum and instruction (school-district level), director of curriculum and instruction, associate superintendent of schools, and finally superintendent of schools.

Along the way, this educator picked up additional responsibilities and education, which helped prepare her for the next level. This included serving as a chairperson of the social studies department at her high school, coordinating the self-study process required for the school to renew its accreditation, and going to school at night and during the summers to complete a master's degree and eventually a doctorate in educational administration.

The president of a medium-sized four-year college began his career as an instructor. In time he advanced to positions of increasing responsibility, including assistant professor, associate professor, department chairperson, assistant vice president of instruction, and vice president of instruction, until he reached the pinnacle of his career as president of the college.

While progressing, when he was promoted to full professor, he took on several special assignments in areas such as developing new academic programs, directing grant-funded projects, and completing an intensive summer program for educational administrators.

Of course, everyone doesn't follow a "typical" path, and many other possibilities exist. Some administrators come from areas outside of education, where they have gained management expertise. For example, a former military officer, business executive, or manager in a nonprofit organization might switch to education. Likewise, a teacher or other employee might take on a management position without having held a number of other administrative jobs.

In some cases, an educator's entire educational experience may have taken place in a single organization, advancing from one position to the next over the years. For others, the career path may include working at one school or college for a while, and then moving to another. Quite often, executive managers have had substantial experience at several institutions.

At the same time, the great majority of administrative positions are at levels other than executive administration. For every college president or vice president, there are dozens of other managers. These managers direct activities such as business affairs, physical facilities, fund-raising, and student affairs. They coordinate departments in a wide range of activities or supervise personnel in various support units. The same is true in school districts or other organizations. Among other things, this means job opportunities may be open to younger or less experienced candidates than those eligible for senior-level positions.

In elementary and secondary schools, administrative employment areas include: school-level administration, which consists of primarily principals and assistant principals; general district-level administration, such as superintendents and assistant superintendents; financial administration; logistical support; facilities management; public information/community relations; athletic administration; administration of guidance, counseling, and related support services; and special program administration.

In colleges and universities, there is a wide range of administrative areas in which jobs can be found, including:

admissions and registration
alumni affairs
association administration
athletics
business and financial management
computer services and information technology
conference planning and administration
counseling
development and institutional advancement
executive management
extension services
facilities management
financial aid
grants administration or grant development
human resources administration
institutional research
medical and health administration
minority affairs
residential life
security and campus safety
student services

REPRESENTATIVE
ADMINISTRATIVE POSITIONS

While administrative positions share common responsibilities as previously noted, each administrative role also carries its own specific duties. Following is an overview of several representative roles.

Principals and Assistant Principals

Perhaps the most widely known role in educational administration is that of the principal. Men and women who hold this position, or that of assistant principal, play a central role in the educational world. They manage the day-to-day operations of schools, serving as on-site supervisors of teachers and other personnel. They are in charge of a variety of areas ranging from student discipline to parent relations. In the process, they serve as the leaders of any school.

A look at actual position descriptions for these educational administrators can be revealing. Following is a job description for a high school principal with the Gary Community School Corporation in Gary, Indiana.

PRINCIPAL—SECONDARY (HIGH SCHOOL)

Qualifications:

> The principal will possess a master's degree in education or educational administration from an accredited college or university as well as an Indiana Secondary Administrative/ Supervisory License. Also required are a minimum of five years of successful teaching experience at the secondary level, previous administrative/supervisory experience,

knowledge of secondary education curriculum and instruction techniques, demonstrated effective verbal and written communication skills, and the ability to establish and maintain effective working relationships with employees, students, parents, and the public.

Job Goal:

To use leadership, supervisory, and administrative skills to promote the educational development of each student. Administers and coordinates curriculum and instruction for the assigned school; supervises and evaluates programs and activities; establishes standards and expectations for assigned school; and communicates with school community.

Duties:

Administers and coordinates curriculum and instruction for the assigned school.

Establishes and maintains an effective learning climate in the school.

Supervises and evaluates programs and activities.

Develops and implements effective school/community relationships.

Initiates, designs, and implements programs to meet specific needs of the school.

Prepares and conducts staff development activities.

Establishes and implements policies and procedures for the assigned school.

Makes recommendations concerning the school's administration and instruction.

Prepares and administers the school budget and supervises school finances.

Supervises the maintenance of all required building records and reports.

Prepares or supervises the preparation of reports, records, lists, and all other paperwork required or appropriate to the school's administration.

Works with various members of the central administrative staff on school problems of more than in-school import, such as transportation and special services.

Keeps supervisor informed of events and activities of an unusual nature as well as routine matters related to the supervisor's accountability.

Interprets and enforces district policies and administrative regulations.

Maintains active relationships with students and parents.

Performs related duties as assigned by supervisor.

Assistant principals perform similar duties, but they serve under the supervision of a principal. In addition, they may be assigned distinct roles such as student discipline or class scheduling.

In order to give you an idea of what life is like on the job, you should know what the typical responsibilities are of an assistant principal. On any given day you might find yourself assisting in developing and coordinating curriculum and instruction at the individual school level; supervising the attendance and discipline of students; supervising the management and care of school buildings and facilities; and providing leadership in supervising and evaluating programs and activities. Not to be forgotten, you might also need to prepare written reports, help to promote effective community relationships, assist in establishing and carrying out school goals and objectives, and perform other tasks under the supervision of the principal.

The U.S. Department of Labor describes the duties for an assistant principal as follows:

Administers school student personnel program in primary or secondary school, and counsels and disciplines students, performing any combination of following tasks: Formulates student personnel policies, such as code of ethics. Plans and supervises school student activity programs. Gives individual and group guidance for personal problems, educational and vocational objectives, and social and recreational activities. Talks with and disciplines students in cases of attendance and behavior problems. Supervises students in attendance at assemblies and athletic events. Walks about school building and property to monitor safety and security or directs and coordinates teacher supervision of areas such as halls and cafeteria. Observes and evaluates teacher performance. Maintains records of student attendance. Arranges for and oversees substitute teachers. Works with administrators to coordinate and supervise student teacher programs. Teaches courses. Assists principal to interview and hire teachers. Organizes and administers in-service teacher training. Acts as principal in absence of principal. May be required to have certification from state.

Superintendents and District-Level Administrators

While principals may be in charge of individual schools, other positions deal with the operations of an entire school district. Most schools are part of a larger network of schools organized in a school district or similar arrangement. The chief administrative officer is normally a superintendent of schools or comparable position. Often, this role is supported by one or more associate or assistant superintendents.

Here is the U.S. Department of Labor's description of the school superintendent's role:

Directs and coordinates activities concerned with administration of city, county, or other school system in accordance with board of education standards. Formulates plans and policies for educational program and submits them to school board for approval. Administers program for selection of school sites, construction of buildings, and provision of equipment and supplies. Directs preparation and presentation of school budget and determines amount of school bond issues required to finance educational program. Addresses community and civic groups to enlist their support. Interprets program and policies of school system to school personnel, to individuals and community groups, and to governmental agencies. Coordinates work of school system with related activities of other school districts and agencies. May ensure that laws applying to attendance of children at school are enforced. May supervise examining, appointing, training, and promotion of teaching personnel. May specialize in areas such as personnel services, curriculum development, or business administration.

In addition to school superintendents, other administrators work behind the scenes in school district central offices. These administrators employ a variety of skills and educational backgrounds to keep things running smoothly. They might direct subject area programs such as math, English, or vocational education; oversee counseling and testing programs and services; coordinate school psychology services; provide oversight and support in various areas of curriculum and instruction; and coordinate professional development activities. Other responsibilities might include providing grant writing services and overseeing grants management efforts, directing transportation services, coordinating facilities maintenance and construction services, overseeing fiscal affairs, and coordinating public information and community relations efforts.

Related Administrative Positions

Although most positions in educational administration are found at the school or district level, others also support the overall educational enterprise. These include the state superintendent of schools, state-level administrators in specific areas of responsibility (such as curriculum and instruction or financial management), administrators of educational associations, managers in the U.S. Department of Education or other government agencies, and administrators in regional service agencies or other organizations.

Postsecondary Educational Administrators

"Postsecondary" refers to education beyond the high school level. Colleges, universities, and other postsecondary schools enroll more than twelve million students every year at the undergraduate level, and more than two million in graduate or professional studies.

That is a lot of students! To meet their educational needs, nearly five thousand institutions now operate in the United States and Canada. These schools, in turn, employ large numbers of people not only to teach, but to provide a host of services ranging from administration to counseling.

According to the *Chronicle of Higher Education,* U.S. colleges and universities employ more than five-hundred thousand full-time faculty members. But at most colleges, full-time faculty represent less than half of all employees. Other employment categories, covered in later chapters, include counselors, student support personnel, librarians, technical specialists and paraprofessionals, clerical staff, and maintenance and custodial workers.

All told, in fact, more than one million people are employed in nonfaculty positions in postsecondary institutions. They range from support roles such as custodians and food service workers to top-level managers. Supervising other personnel and coordinating the many activities undertaken in colleges and universities is the responsibility of various educational administrators.

Typical titles for such positions, in order of responsibility, include the following:

President
Academic Vice President
Associate Vice President
Business Manager
Dean of Academic Affairs
Academic Division Chair
Director of Development
Director of Continuing Education
Project Coordinator

The top-level job in most colleges and universities is that of president. Certainly the odds of becoming a president are lower than for those of most other positions, since there is usually just one president per college, and both the basic requirements and the level of competition in being selected are stiff. But well over three-thousand men and women serve in such roles, and aspiring to a presidency can be a reasonable goal for the highly motivated education professional.

Here is the Department of Labor's description of this job role:

PRESIDENT—ALTERNATE TITLE: CHANCELLOR

Formulates plans and programs for and directs administration of college, school, or university, within authority delegated by governing board. Confers with board of control to plan and initiate programs concerning organizational, operational, and academic functions of campus, and oversees their execution. Administers fiscal and physical planning activities, such as development of budget and building expansion programs, and recommends their adoption. Negotiates with administrative officials and representatives of business, community, and civic groups to promote educational, research, and public service objectives and policies of institution as formulated by board of control. Establishes operational procedures, rules, and standards relating to faculty and staff classification standards, financial disbursements, and accounting requirements. Represents campus on board of control and at formal functions.

Another important role is that of the chief academic officer within an institution. Following is a description of a typical such leadership position as noted in the Department of Labor's *Dictionary of Occupational Titles:*

ACADEMIC DEAN—ALTERNATE TITLES: ACADEMIC VICE PRESIDENT, DEAN OF INSTRUCTION, FACULTY DEAN, PROVOST, UNIVERSITY DEAN, VICE PRESIDENT FOR INSTRUCTION

Develops academic policies and programs for college or university. Directs and coordinates activities of deans and chairpersons of individual colleges. Advises on personnel matters. Determines scheduling of courses and recommends implementation of additional courses. Coordinates activities of student advisors. Participates in activities of faculty committees, and in development of academic budget. Advises president, educational institution on academic matters. Serves as liaison officer with accrediting agencies that evaluate academic programs. May serve as chief administrative officer in absence of president. May provide general direction to librarian, director of admissions, and registrar.

Another important role is that of department head or department chairperson. (In a university, a similar role with broad-based responsibilities is that of dean of a college within the university, such as a college of arts and sciences, engineering, or business.) Persons holding these roles administer the affairs of one of more academic departments or support areas in a college or university. In an academic area such as history, foreign languages, or engineering, this might include duties such as arranging class schedules, assigning faculty to teach classes, recruiting and hiring new faculty, managing departmental budgets, and, in some cases, teaching.

Here is a position description for the Dean of the College of Business at Ball State University in Indiana:

DEAN

Reporting:

Reports to the Provost and Vice President for Academic Affairs.

Role:

Serves as the chief academic and administrative officer of the College.

Responsibilities:

Major responsibilities include providing leadership in the development and evaluation of excellence in teaching, scholarly productivity, service, strategic planning, and in securing external gifts, grants, and funding; encouraging the continuous improvement of management education; acting as fiscal agent for the college; serving as primary spokesperson to the business community; providing leadership in integrating the management of technology into college programs; and providing leadership for business, economic development, and management education on local, state, regional, national, and global bases.

Minimum Qualifications:

The person in this position will need to have earned a doctorate in an appropriate field from an accredited institution of higher learning, at least five years of experience as a full-time university faculty member/administrator, the ability to communicate effectively, knowledge and understanding of business and its role in society, and a record of success in teaching and published research in refereed journals that will merit a faculty appointment in one of the departments of the college at the rank of professor with tenure.

Although academics constitute the core of a college, other functions are also important. For example, every college and university operates a business office or similar office to collect tuition, coordinate purchasing functions, manage the institution's overall budget, and perform other important functions. Representative position titles in this area include:

Associate Vice Chancellor for Business Affairs
Associate Vice President of Business Affairs
Chief Financial Officer
Compliance Services Manager
Dean of Business Affairs
Director of Purchasing
Financial Manager
Internal Audit Manager
Internal Auditor
Purchasing Officer
Vice President, Administrative and Business Services
Vice President for Business and Finance

Though a doctorate may be required for the chief business officer's role in some universities, in many colleges a master's degree or less will be sufficient. In fact, that is a major difference between many support positions outside of academic affairs and those more directly connected with instruction.

Other administrative support roles (some discussed in more detail in later chapters) include vice presidents, deans, directors, coordinators, and other managers in areas such as institutional advancement or development, facilities management, human resources, workforce development, continuing education, economic development, public affairs, computing and information technology, and others.

ONE DAY ON THE JOB

Obviously, with so many types of administrative positions, there is probably no such thing as an "average" day on the job for an educational administrator. But the following schedule illustrates what one day's work might involve for an experienced academic manager in a collegiate setting:

8:30 A.M.   Arrive at office; return phone calls from previous afternoon; read and respond to E-mail messages.

9:00   Attend budget meeting with managers from other departments.

11:00   Meet with two faculty members to review preliminary grant proposal.

11:45   Read the day's mail; prepare responses.

12:30 P.M.   Attend luncheon meeting with job candidate and search committee.

1:45   Meet with student newspaper reporter who is doing a story on efforts to obtain funds for a new campus building.

2:30   Sign purchase requisitions, memos, and other documents; read draft report on academic program review.

3:00   Meet with institutional research officer regarding report required by state agency.

3:30   Work on correspondence.

4:00   Call community leaders regarding a chamber of commerce project; work on speech to be given at student awards dinner.

5:30   End of day.

On another day, work might not end at this time, but might include attending a dinner meeting or an evening cultural event. Or time might be spent teaching a class, playing in a charity golf tournament, or traveling to a conference or meeting with other educators. Some mornings may start later, especially after a commitment the previous evening, and the total hours worked in any one week may vary.

CHAPTER 3

COUNSELORS AND STUDENT SERVICE SPECIALISTS

There is no doubt about it, education is a helping enterprise. The primary goal of those working in education is to help students learn, eventually preparing them to assume productive roles in society.

Outside the confines of the classroom, students at all levels need help in a variety of ways. From choosing academic programs or classes to dealing with personal problems, students often desire assistance. Providing such help is the domain of counselors and other appropriately trained personnel. They play a key role in helping students succeed.

Although counseling and student support jobs can be challenging, they are not for everyone. If you are an introverted type who would rather work on a computer or complete paperwork than talk at length with a student or help someone overcome problems or make plans, this may not be a realistic career area to pursue. But for those who truly enjoy interacting with others, it can be a promising career path.

COUNSELORS AND SCHOOL PSYCHOLOGISTS

In schools and colleges, counselors work with students in a variety of areas from dealing with personal problems to making career choices. In high schools, counselors advise students on applying to college, choosing majors, seeking financial aid, pursuing noncollegiate career plans, and other matters. They also may help students deal with personal challenges ranging from academic growth to substance abuse.

Counselors who work in elementary schools observe younger children, evaluate special needs or potential, and confer with teachers and parents. They do not emphasize vocational planning as much as do high school counselors, but they may help students develop good study habits and social skills.

At both levels, they work with individual students and also with groups. They try to help students deal with domestic problems and other challenges. Sometimes they administer tests or help coordinate special activities.

A related role is that of school psychologists. These professionals assess psychological needs of students and provide services to help meet their needs.

Here is a position description for such a position at Milton Hershey School, a private school in Pennsylvania:

SCHOOL PSYCHOLOGIST

Responsibilities:

The School Psychologist is responsible for enriching the experiences of students by facilitating their best possible adjustment to school through a program of psychological services, including assessment, consultations, intervention, and collaboration within the school community.

Qualifications:

Individuals in this position will possess a master's degree in school psychology from an APA-approved program; state psychology licensure and/or school certification (or licensure eligible); a minimum of three years successful psychotherapy/psychology experience with children and adolescents; commitment to and support for all students and adults in a diverse multicultural environment; knowledge and experience in psychological/diagnostic testing therapeutic techniques, crisis intervention, and medication/treatment plan management; the ability to establish professional rapport with students, staff, and parents/sponsors; excellent interpersonal, organizational, and communication skills; and working knowledge of personal computers.

COLLEGE AND UNIVERSITY STUDENT AFFAIRS

In colleges and universities, a variety of positions are involved in working directly with students. Counselors at this level perform many functions not unlike those of secondary school counselors, but often with a more specialized approach depending on the type of position held. For example, a career counselor may help students plan for careers after college as well as choose vocations, while a crisis counselor may deal with problems ranging from substance abuse to depression. Typical job titles in the counseling area include:

Assistant Director of Counseling
Career Counselor
Counseling Coordinator
Counseling and Student Advising Specialist
Counselor
Crisis Counselor
Director of Career Services
Staff Counselor

One example of a specialized counseling position is that of career counselor. If you are working as a career counselor, on any given day you might find yourself providing counseling services designed to enhance job search outcomes of students, alumni, or others; planning and implementing programs and services in resume skills, interview techniques, and other job search areas; researching employer needs and communicating openings with the campus community; coordinating job fairs, interviews, or other related activities; facilitating skill building and networking services; collecting information for evaluation of graduates' workplace performance; or performing other duties related to helping students or others pursue career goals.

Other positions serve specific groups of students. Here is a description for a foreign student adviser from the U.S. Department of Labor's *Dictionary of Occupational Titles:*

FOREIGN STUDENT ADVISER

Assists foreign students in making academic, personal-social, and environmental adjustment to campus and community life. Evaluates students' qualifications in light of admission requirements and makes recommendations relative to admission. Develops and maintains case histories, noting language, educational, social, religious, or physical problems affecting students' adjustments. Provides informal counseling and orientation regarding recreational and religious outlets, study habits, and personal adjustments. Interprets university regulations and requirements. Assists students in complying with government regulations concerning status, immigration, visas, passports, permission to work, and related matters. Represents students in cases involving conflict with regulations. Cooperates with other personnel service bureaus to assist in adjustment of students. Approves students' proposed budgets and requests release of funds from students' home governments to meet financial obligations. Recommends students for scholarships, grants-in-aid, and waivers-of-tuition fees on basis of scholarship, character, and financial need. Encourages and coordinates activities of groups that promote understanding of foreign cultures. May assist in curriculum planning.

In addition to counseling, colleges and universities offer a variety of services for students that require the attention of staff assigned to perform such tasks. The overall area providing this kind of support may be referred to as student services, student affairs, or a similar designation.

Just some of the areas student services staff may deal with include: overall student development, minority concerns, financial aid, housing, admissions, career planning, registration, student activities, international student services, tutoring, personal counseling, and crisis counseling. These and similar areas form the focus for the work of a variety of jobs in student services. Such positions range from entry-level jobs to high-level administrative roles.

Student Services Leadership Roles

Most colleges have one or more leadership positions in student services such as dean of students, vice president for student services, or similar positions.

Here is a position description for such a role at the University of Wyoming:

DEAN OF STUDENTS

Responsibilities:

The Dean of Students provides visionary leadership and direction to programs and services that promote student involvement, learning, and academic success. He or she reports to the Vice President of Student Affairs and collaborates with faculty, academic departments, and student leaders.

Duties:

> The Dean directs, develops, or provides referrals to programs and services that enhance the overall quality of the student experience and each student's potential for success, with special emphasis on the concerns of freshmen. He or she provides leadership for the Office of Student Life, which includes a range of student life functions that promote civility, support an inclusive campus climate and community, and celebrate diversity. This position also provides advisement and consultation on student issues and concerns, conflict resolution and ombudsman services, student due process, and appeals. The Dean oversees nine fraternities and four sororities and advises and supervises the fiscal and staff issues of the Associated Students of the University of Wyoming (ASUW) and Student Publications.

Qualifications:

> Qualifications for this position include a master's degree—doctorate preferred in higher education, student personnel, counseling, or related field; a record of collaboration with faculty to provide educational programs and services to increase student success and retention; at least five years of increasing administrative experience with budgets and personnel management, preferably as an assistant/associate or director in student affairs; excellent communication, conflict resolution, and problem-solving skills; experience in crisis management; and a demonstrated commitment to diversity.

Following is an example of a leadership position in this area at California's San Bernardino Community College District:

DEAN OF COUNSELING/STUDENT DEVELOPMENT

Duties:

Under the general direction of the Vice President of Student Services, the Dean of Counseling/Student Development supervises the Department Chair of Counseling; Counseling Faculty Members; the Matriculation Coordinator; the Transfer Center Director; the Articulation Officer; and several other positions. Supervision and direction provided by the Dean ensures program development and the highest quality of service to students.

Working with the Dean of Student Support Services and Enrollment Management, the Dean of Counseling/Student Development is also responsible for planning, organizing, and coordinating the International Student Services and outreach and recruitment activities with high schools.

Minimum Qualifications:

A master's degree from an accredited institution of higher education, at least three years of experience as a supervisor in the area of counseling/student development, and experience that indicates a sensitivity to and an understanding of the diverse academic, socioeconomic, cultural, disability, and ethnic backgrounds of community college students and personnel are required.

Student Activities Positions

A more focused position without a high degree of management duties involves working directly with students in extracurricular activities. Here is a description for the position of coordinator of student activities at Rogers State University in Oklahoma:

COORDINATOR OF STUDENT ACTIVITIES

Duties:

The Coordinator provides primary leadership for the development and implementation of comprehensive cocurricular programs that focus on student involvement, skill building, and the manifestation of the University's missions and goals. The Coordinator manages daily operations of the student activities office while maintaining high levels of student contact, including supervision of the student union, student information center, and advising student groups.

Qualifications:

A bachelor's degree is required; student activity experience is preferred along with excellent communication skills and experience with leadership programming.

Financial Aid Staff

Another important job area deals with student financial aid. Following is a U.S. Department of Labor description of a financial aid director.

FINANCIAL AID DIRECTOR—ALTERNATE TITLES: DIRECTOR OF FINANCIAL AID AND PLACEMENTS, DIRECTOR OF STUDENT AID

Directs scholarship, grant-in-aid, and loan programs to provide financial assistance to students in college or university. Selects candidates and determines types and amounts of aid. Organizes and oversees student financial counseling activities. Coordinates activities with other departmental staff engaged in issuing or collecting student payments. May teach. May select financial aid candidates as members of committee and be designated Chairperson, Scholarship and Loan Committee.

Student Housing Positions

For a beginning-level experience in higher education, a good place to start is working as a resident assistant or residence hall director. These types of positions involve helping supervise students living in dormitories or other college-sponsored housing.

Here is an example of such a position in a large public university:

GRADUATE ASSISTANT HALL DIRECTOR

Overall Role:

The Graduate Assistant Hall Director assists with the administrative management and programming functions of a university residence hall serving three hundred to four hundred undergraduate students and fosters living/learning communities conducive to the personal growth and academic success of the resident student.

Hours:

20–25 hours per week during the academic year.

Responsibilities:

Responsibilities of the Graduate Assistant Hall Director include assisting the Director with the selection and direction of eight-to-twelve member student personnel staff; planning and implementing educational and social programming in connection with the Hall Council; advising and counseling residents; performing administrative tasks in connection with the management of the facility; and performing on-call duties.

Qualifications:

A bachelor's degree is preferred. Residence hall living experience as well as residence hall staff experience are considered very helpful. A major in counseling, sociology, or a related field and graduate hours in student personnel, counseling, sociology, or a related field are also helpful.

Other related positions include director of student housing, housing coordinator, residential life coordinator, and similar roles.

Positions in Athletics

For those interested in sports, several types of positions involve managing and supporting athletic programs. These include jobs such as sports information director, coach, athletic director, and various assistant-level roles.

A description of the job of athletic director, taken from the *Dictionary of Occupational Titles,* is as follows:

ATHLETIC DIRECTOR

Plans, administers, and directs intercollegiate athletic activities in college or university. Interprets and participates in formulating extramural athletic policies. Employs and discharges coaching staff and other department employees on own initiative or at direction of board in charge of athletics. Directs preparation and dissemination of publicity to promote athletic events. Plans and coordinates activities of coaching staff. Prepares budget and authorizes department expenditures. Plans and schedules sports events, and oversees ticket sales activities. Certifies reports of income produced from ticket sales. May direct programs for students of physical education.

Types and levels of jobs in athletics vary widely. In a small college, the overall staff in this area may be quite small. In larger institutions, athletic departments may be much larger. In sheer numbers they offer greater opportunity, but there may also be more competition among those seeking jobs.

Admissions and Registration Staff

In every institution someone must help prospective students apply for admission, maintain records related to admission, process grades and transcript information, maintain each student's academic record, and perform other related tasks. Personnel who work in admissions and records, enrollment management, registration, or similar areas carry out such duties.

Job titles in the area of admissions and registration include:

Assistant Registrar
Associate Director of Admissions
Chief Admissions Officer
Dean of Admissions
Director of Admissions
Director of Enrollment Management
Director of Enrollment and Registration Services
Director of Graduate Admissions
Director of Outreach Programs
Director of Undergraduate Admissions
Minority Recruiter
Recruiter
Registrar
Vice President of Enrollment Management

A good entry-level position for those interested in working in this area is a job as a recruiter, admissions counselor, or admissions representative. Here is a description for an admissions representative at the University of Rochester:

ADMISSIONS REPRESENTATIVE

Duties:

The Recruiter for the University will visit public and private secondary schools for the purpose of discussing the University with and interpreting the University to interested students, parents, and guidance personnel. He or she will represent the University at College Nights and College Conferences, addressing groups of students, parents, and guidance personnel; will coordinate these visits with alumni and other volunteers in travel area; and will interview applicants throughout the year. The Recruiter will respond to telephone and written inquiries from prospective students, parents, and guidance counselors regarding specifics of University programs and policies; participate in special on-campus functions for prospective students, parents, and counselors, such as prospective student receptions and counselor programs; and develop and maintain current knowledge of financial aid for purposes of informing students, parents, and counselors. He or she will also review and evaluate all types of applications for admission and serve as a voting member of the Committee on Admissions.

Qualifications:

Qualifications include a bachelor's degree, or an equivalent combination of education and experience.

DO YOU HAVE WHAT IT TAKES TO SUCCEED IN STUDENT SERVICES?

Basic requirements in this area include, for most jobs, a bachelor's or master's degree and in some elementary and secondary positions, state certification. In addition, those working in counseling or student services will need excellent oral communication skills, a genuine liking for people and a concern for their problems and needs, and the ability to work in teams as well as in one-on-one situations. A high energy level, a sense of discretion, and a personality that others find trustworthy are also very important. Finally you must be able to follow policies and guidelines and plan and implement goals with creativity and excellent problem-solving abilities. Overall, a commitment to supporting instructional programs is paramount.

If you possess many of these traits, you might find great job satisfaction and career success in this field.

QUESTIONS TO ASK YOURSELF

If the possibility of working in counseling or student services sounds appealing, ask yourself questions such as these: Do I enjoy talking and working closely with other people? Do I have excellent skills in oral communication? Do I have empathy for others? Would I be comfortable listening to others express their problems, needs, or goals? Can I work independently without direct supervision? Can I be dependable in following specific policies and guidelines? Am I willing to obtain the necessary training or academic preparation to prepare for a job in this field? Am I competent at using a personal computer or other office equipment? Can I see myself working in an educational environment? If you answered "yes" to most of these questions, you may be well suited to working in counseling or student services.

CHAPTER 4

LIBRARIANS AND MEDIA SPECIALISTS

LIBRARIES OF TODAY

Schools and libraries go hand in hand. Although some libraries exist independently of schools and colleges, the converse is seldom true. Almost every school maintains one or more libraries. This might range from a modest learning center in a small elementary school to a huge university library boasting millions of books, periodicals, and other materials.

In order to operate, libraries need appropriate staffing. Professional librarians and a variety of support staff meet this demand. The overall category of library personnel represents a special niche within the world of education, and one that provides a variety of career opportunities.

The library of the twenty-first century can be an exciting workplace. Along with traditional books, magazines, and journals, it serves as a repository or linkage point for a variety of electronic media. Today, even the smallest library can provide connections to a mind-boggling array of information resources. Thanks to the power of the Internet and the availability of high-capacity electronic storage media, a modest school library can provide resources for students that not long ago would have been unavailable, in some cases not even in the world's largest libraries.

If your primary concept of library work involves checking out books to patrons, you might want to expand your vision. Modern librarians are just as likely to be helping students learn to use electronic databases as keeping track of books or other types of printed material.

Major functions of librarians and related positions include administering libraries and performing related library services; selecting, acquiring, cataloging, classifying, circulating, and maintaining library materials; providing reference, bibliographical, and reader's advisory services; and managing, maintaining, and providing assistance with electronically stored information.

Educational requirements for library positions vary depending on the type of employer and the level of responsibility. For many positions, a bachelor's degree is a minimum requirement. For others, including a large number of college and university positions, a master's degree from an institution accredited by the American Library Association is expected. For more details regarding educational options, see Chapter 7.

COLLEGE LIBRARY POSITIONS

Following are typical titles for library-related positions at the college level:

Assistant Director for Collections
Assistant Librarian
Associate Dean of Libraries
Bibliographic Control Librarian
Cataloger
College Archivist

Coordinator for Bibliographic and Digital Services
Coordinator of Library Instruction
Curator of Rare Books and Manuscripts
Dean of Libraries and Media Services
Dean of the Library
Digital Library Director
Director of Library
Director of Library/Learning Resources
Electronic Resources Librarian
Government Documents and Electronic Resources Librarian
Head, Catalog Department
Head, Collections Services
Humanities and Social Sciences Librarian
Instructional Services Librarian
Librarian
Manuscripts Cataloger
Mathematics Librarian
Physical and Applied Sciences Bibliographer
Public Services Librarian
Serials and Receiving Unit Head
University Reserves Librarian

In colleges and universities, some library positions involve specializing in a designated academic area. One librarian may specialize in history or the social sciences, while another might focus on the natural sciences.

Following is an example of a position description for a librarian specializing in music at Haverford College in Pennsylvania.

MUSIC LIBRARIAN

Overall Responsibility:

Planning, developing, managing, and evaluating the facilities, services, and resources of music collections.

Specific Duties:

Administers or performs all operations of a departmental Music Library, including course reserves, circulation, and stack maintenance.

Hires, trains, schedules, and supervises the Music Library's student assistants.

Develops and manages the music collection in all formats; stays current with developments in musicology, music theory, composition, and performance; coordinates collection development with other cooperating colleges.

Provides a full range of music reference and instructional services to the campus community including research assistance and bibliographic instruction both in and out of the classroom. Creates instructional materials in support of public service functions.

Works with the technical services staff to catalog scores, recordings, monographs, and serials.

Introduces new technologies necessary to the study of music and plans for the improvement of Music Library facilities.

Assumes responsibility for collection development and library research instruction in other subject areas as needed.

Contributes to cooperative projects of a three-college consortium through membership on-task forces or committees.

Basic Requirements:

Experience with music resources and services in an academic library and supervisory experience, preferably with student assistants, is required. Academic or public library experience in reference services, user instruction, collection development, and music cataloging, and experience in the design, implementation, and use of digital resources and instructional technologies are highly preferred.

ALA-accredited master's degree or its equivalent in training and experience is required. Degree in music and academic background in modern languages and literatures or in the social sciences are highly preferred.

Familiarity with a wide range of music genres and a general background in musicology, music theory, composition, and performance; knowledge of or the ability to learn the informational/instructional technologies and equipment associated with academic libraries; highly developed interpersonal, communication, and teaching skills; evidence of strong commitment to teamwork and service; work-related evidence of independence, creativity, flexibility, and resourcefulness; and evidence of commitment to the purposes and goals of a liberal arts education also are necessary. Must be willing to maintain a flexible schedule; some night and weekend hours are possible.

Following is an example of another academically focused library position. This job covers the humanities and social sciences at the library at the University of North Texas.

HUMANITIES AND SOCIAL SCIENCES LIBRARIAN

Duties:

Serves as one of six librarians who provide reference and informational assistance at the General Reference Desk, through the Online Reference Help Desk, and through individual reference consultations. As part of this team, the librarian's schedule requires at least one evening a week as well as participation in a weekend rotation. The librarian conducts library instruction sessions, serves as liaison to one or more academic departments, prepares web pages and other bibliographic resources, and participates actively in collection development and collection evaluation. He or she also provides staff training and performs other duties as assigned.

Required Qualifications:

An ALA-accredited master's degree or its equivalent, a bachelor's degree in one of the humanities or social sciences, working knowledge of reference sources, both print and electronic, good verbal and written communication skills and good interpersonal skills, the ability to work successfully in a team environment, and a strong commitment to public service are required. Additional qualifications, including two years of academic reference experience, are preferred.

A beginning library position would involve lower-level duties and at the same time, require less experience. A position as a library assistant, library technician, or similar role can be a good starting point.

Here is a description for such a position in a university library. In this case, the job focuses on audiovisual services, but in other similar jobs the focus might be on traditional book collections, periodicals, or other areas.

LIBRARY ASSISTANT

Duties:

The Library Assistant will explain and interpret policies and procedures to users, schedule the use of audiovisual equipment, assist with accounting and processing of orders and selection of film and videos and supervise their use, coordinate delivery and pickup service, assist with microprinters, and catalog nonprint materials, maintain database, and input records.

Minimum Qualifications:

A high school diploma (or GED), six months' experience in a library or equivalent, and experience in a public service capacity are necessary. An associate degree or technical/ vocational training in Library Science or Media and experience in a media environment including audiovisual and microfilm/microfiche equipment are preferred.

Other positions focus on specific tasks such as cataloging or providing reference services. Following is a description for a cataloger's position:

CATALOGER

Responsibilities:

The Cataloger performs original and complex copy cataloging for a variety of formats and in all subject areas, maintains bibliographic and authority records, establishes name and series authority records, assists in analyzing and evaluating processes and in helping departmental staff stay current on emerging trends in technical services, helps resolve complex problems surrounding cataloging issues, and represents the campus on committees charged with developing and enforcing cataloging standards.

Qualifications:

A master's degree from an ALA-accredited institution and familiarity with the appropriate formats and cataloging tools and standard practices are required.

Virtually every college and university employs librarians and library staff. The number might vary from a few in a small community college or four-year school to scores or more in the largest academic libraries. For those with the necessary credentials, career potential can be promising.

SCHOOL LIBRARIANS

In a high school or middle school setting, librarians may be designated by a variety of job titles. With the added emphasis on electronic collections in addition to traditional books and magazines, a frequent title is Media Specialist. Other titles include:

Coordinator, Media Center
Director, Media Center
Learning Resources Director
Library Director
School Librarian

Here is the U.S. Department of Labor's description for such a position:

> Assesses and meets needs of students and faculty for information, and develops programs to stimulate students' interests in reading and use of types of resources. Selects and organizes books, films, tapes, recordings, and other materials and equipment. Suggests appropriate books to students for classroom assignments and personal readings. Plans and carries out program of instruction in use by school library media center. Prepares and administers budget for media center. Confers with faculty to provide materials for classroom instruction. Confers with parents, faculty, public librarians, and community organizations to develop programs to enrich students' communications skills. Reviews records to compile lists of overdue materials and notifies borrowers to arrange for their return.

Media Specialist

A number of skills or competencies are needed for success as a library media specialist. Among them are an appropriate educational background such as a master's degree or a specialization within another degree program in library and information science, classroom teaching experience, the ability to work cooperatively with others, good communication and organizational skills, and the ability to train others.

In recent years, an additional area of emphasis for many school librarians is the use of computers. In modern schools, librarians often maintain computers that are used by students for bibliographic work or online communications. This may involve use of the Internet for instructional purposes.

In large schools, more than one librarian or media specialist may be employed. In smaller schools, one such position may be charged with coordinating all of the library's activities.

A related position is that of library aide, media aide, or similar position. A paraprofessional position of this type does not require the same educational level as does a professional librarian, and the work performed falls under the supervision of a librarian or media center director.

DO YOU HAVE WHAT IT TAKES TO SUCCEED IN A LIBRARY CAREER?

The most fundamental requirement for a library career is the knowledge gained by completion of appropriate educational programs. A master's degree from an institution accredited by the American Library Association is a common requirement, although it may not be needed for some types of positions.

In a university environment, training in a specific academic area (such as history, foreign languages, chemistry, or some other discipline taught at a given institution) may also be needed.

Additional skills are similar to those expected in other education-related careers. Typically, they include strong organizational skills, attention to detail, a love of books and other informational materials, a willingness to help others in locating information, the ability to communicate well both orally and in writing, a dependable work style and strong work ethic, enthusiasm for one's work, good computer skills, a willingness to pursue additional training as needed. Also desirable is a strong sense of commitment to the employing institution, including a sense of teamwork that goes beyond the library and includes the school, college, or other employing organization.

QUESTIONS TO ASK YOURSELF

In considering the possibility of a library career in an educational setting, ask yourself questions such as the following: Can I picture myself working in a library? Do I enjoy spending time in libraries? Do I have good organizational skills? Do I enjoy working with people? Would I be good at assisting students, faculty, or other patrons in one-on-one or small group settings? Do I have solid oral communication skills? Good writing skills? Am I adept at using computers? Am I good at working with details? Do I work well without a great deal of direct supervision? Am I willing to obtain additional training to gain skills and knowledge in specialized library or media applications? Am I good at following through on details and keeping accurate records? Do I have the right kind of personality to work in a library setting on a long-term basis? Would I enjoy providing library support within a school, college, or other educational organization?

A positive response to most or all of these questions is a good indicator of at least some potential in the educational library area. For those with the right interests and skills, this can be a rewarding career area within the overall educational setting.

CHAPTER 5

PUBLIC RELATIONS
AND ADVANCEMENT OFFICERS

For any educational institution, an important function is generating support from alumni, the local community, government agencies, private donors, and others who may be in a position to support the school's goals and needs. This may range from writing news releases for submission to newspapers and radio and television stations to conducting large-scale fund-raising programs.

Carrying out such efforts is the role of advancement or public relations personnel. Their area of expertise also may be called development, community relations, or other terms such as:

Annual Fund Coordinator
Assistant Director of Development
Associate Director of Development
Chief Development Officer
Development Coordinator
Development Officer
Director of Corporate and Foundation Relations
Director of Development
Director of Institutional Advancement
Director of Planned Giving

Director of Planning and Grants
Director of Public Information
Grant Writer
Grants Director
Planned Giving Officer
Program Officer
Public Relations Specialist
Vice President for Development
Vice President for Institutional Advancement
Vice President for Resource Development

Those who fill such roles work to garner external support for their institutions. They coordinate fund-raising campaigns; manage development and public relations staff; organize special events; oversee development of publications, advertisements, and other such efforts; or manage efforts in grant proposal development. They maintain contacts with donors and potential donors, write letters, write proposals and reports, develop publicity plans, and perform other related tasks. Some jobs in this area consist of upper- or middle-management positions, while others are clerical or support staff roles. Regardless of the level within an institution, these jobs all contribute to advancing institutions by bringing in funds, promoting a positive public image, or otherwise supporting the school's mission.

Following is a description for a position as Vice President for Advancement at a four-year, state-supported college.

VICE PRESIDENT FOR ADVANCEMENT

Role:

Reporting directly to the President, the Vice President works closely with the President's cabinet and serves as Executive Director of the college's educational foundation.

Responsibilities:

Major responsibilities include planning and directing the college's public relations, alumni, and fund-raising programs.

The Vice President for Advancement also will be closely involved in promoting the college in the areas of alumni affairs, public relations, major gifts, annual fund, planned giving, corporate giving, foundation giving, grants development, and professional development.

Qualifications:

A master's's degree is required; a doctorate is preferred. Four to six years of progressively responsible advancement experience, or similarly transferable work experience, preferably in a college or university environment, are strongly recommended, as are a knowledge of fund-raising techniques and planned giving vehicles, demonstrated ability to work effectively with external constituencies, and excellent communication skills.

Not all positions represent an entire school or college, but instead focus on a single department or unit. Following is a description for such a position at the University of Washington:

PUBLIC INFORMATION SPECIALIST, BIOENGINEERING DEPARTMENT

General Duties:

The major responsibilities of the Public Information Specialist in the Bioengineering Department are to provide professional administrative and operational support to the Department of Bioengineering, working with the Chair, Administrator, and Assistant to the Chair to manage departmental activities and achieve success in reaching departmental mission and goals. Additional duties include overseeing departmental development, including the industrial affiliates program, development correspondence, and gift processing; actively participating as a member of the Bioengineering Curriculum Committee; serving as editor of departmental brochures and the quarterly newsletter; updating and maintaining the department websites; assisting the Chair with special projects; working with the Assistant to the Chair in planning and coordinating major departmental events; assisting the Administrator with facilities and personnel management and special projects; and communicating with the faculty and students to achieve departmental goals.

Requirements:

A bachelor's degree and one year administrative experience, demonstrated writing and editing skills, project management and administrative acumen with a high degree of accuracy and attention to detail, and excellent organizational skills are required. Also necessary are independent judgment and decision-making skills and the desire to work as part of a team, the ability to prioritize work and manage a heavy workload with frequent interruptions, tenacity in meeting deadlines, a working knowledge of appropriate software, the ability to work with issues of a confidential nature using discretion and tact, and strong interpersonal skills to deal with faculty, staff, students, and the University community.

The following position description deals with public relations duties for a single department at Ohio State University:

OUTREACH SPECIALIST

Qualifications:

A bachelor's degree or an equivalent combination of education and experience; experience working in an academic setting in areas of public relations, recruitment, retention, and placement of graduate and undergraduate students; human relations, oral and written communication, and organizational skills are necessary.

Duties:

The Outreach Specialist will assist with the coordination and implementation of public relations, marketing, and student recruitment, retention, and placement efforts; work with other team members to develop placement strategies to assist students in obtaining quality employment; develop a retention process to optimize student graduation rates; initiate innovative programs to significantly increase student enrollment; establish and execute daily activities for the department's marketing plan; and will coordinate representation of the department at designated industry trade shows, educational events, and related events.

Some positions involve working with alumni or other supporters of an institution. Here is a description of a such as position taken from the Department of Labor's *Dictionary of Occupational Titles:*

ALUMNI SECRETARY—ALTERNATE TITLE: DIRECTOR, ALUMNI RELATIONS

Directs and coordinates activities of college or university alumni organization. Communicates with alumni and former students. Organizes and directs alumni organizational functions, regional alumni meetings, and production of alumni publications. Coordinates activities of clerical and publications staff. Promotes alumni endorsement of institutional activities and enlists alumni aid in recruiting students and fund-raising. Secures publicity for alumni functions. May promote athletic events. May assist in follow-up studies of graduates. May supervise alumni field officers.

In private schools and colleges, fund-raising and related tasks may be even more important than in public institutions, since private schools do not receive support from tax dollars. Virtually all private colleges and most private secondary schools employ professionals in the advancement or development area.

Here is a position for a Director of Development at an independent, religious-affiliated secondary school.

DIRECTOR OF DEVELOPMENT

Duties:

> The Director of Development is responsible for the day-to-day operation of the development program. He or she coordinates staff and volunteers in the areas of annual giving, alumni relations, publications, preparation of materials, mailings, fund-raising, and training of volunteers. This position also oversees public relations initiatives, creates and manages the department budget, conducts staff meetings, and coordinates development events.
>
> Specific duties include: creating a development/fund-raising calendar; identifying trends in future donor gifts; developing strategies to fund programs developed by President and Board; coordinating the fund-raising efforts of students and parents; identifying, researching, cultivating, and soliciting major donors; creating programs in which planned giving becomes a viable choice for alumni; conducting and preparing for fund-raising campaigns; identifying and structuring corporate and foundation gifts; developing alumni relations events; and overseeing special events.

Other such positions in elementary and secondary schools may include those such as alumni coordinator, planned giving specialist, or development officer. In public schools, it is less common to find positions specializing in fund-raising. At the district level, such positions may be found, but more typically they also include grant writing or may focus entirely on grant proposal development. Positions focusing on public relations rather than fundraising are more common.

DO YOU HAVE WHAT IT TAKES TO SUCCEED IN ADVANCEMENT AND PUBLIC RELATIONS?

Those who pursue careers in public relations or advancement need to be good communicators as well as diligent workers. Abilities in planning, leading, and presenting information to others are quite important. A typical day on the job might require some or all of the following skills or traits: good or outstanding abilities in oral communication, solid writing skills, skill in working cooperatively with other people, good organizational skills, a solid sense of personal ethics, creativity and problem-solving ability, good analytical skills, a high energy level, a belief in subverting personal gain to overall institutional goals, and an appreciation for, and belief in, the academic mission of the employing school, college, or other organization.

QUESTIONS TO ASK YOURSELF

In considering a possible career in advancement or public relations in an educational setting, ask yourself questions such as these: Am I a hard worker? Do I have good oral communication skills and the willingness to continue improving them? Do I enjoy working with other people in one-on-one or small group situations? Do I have good writing skills? Would I be comfortable taking on a role that includes asking others for contributions? Do others consider me a reliable worker? Am I a good team player? Do I work well independently? Would I be comfortable working in a school or other educational setting? Am I willing to obtain the necessary academic preparation to prepare for a job in this field and to undergo additional training to develop specialized skills if necessary?

If your answer to most or all of these questions is "yes," you may be well suited to a career in educational public relations or advancement. This career area offers great potential for those with the right skills and may be worth investigating further.

CHAPTER 6

ADMINISTRATIVE SUPPORT STAFF AND OTHER SUPPORT JOBS

In any school or other organization, support personnel hold jobs ranging from management to lower-level clerical support functions, maintenance, or other areas of responsibility. Each such role contributes in some way to the overall success of the organization. Both the business manager who oversees financial operations, and the custodian who keeps buildings clean, help an institution meet its primary purpose of educating students.

In this chapter, several types of support positions are described that may not fit into previously discussed categories. Keep in mind that this is by no means an all-inclusive list, but simply a representative look at the variety of positions involved.

For a comprehensive look at employment possibilities at any school district or college, check with its human resources office. In many cases, this information is also available online. Go to www.headhunter.net or www.monsterboard.com to search for positions in this field that are available in an area near you. Additional information on the job search process is provided in Chapter 10.

CLERICAL AND ADMINISTRATIVE
SUPPORT WORKERS

A major employment area in schools and colleges includes clerical personnel and related workers who perform everyday office support functions. Typical titles for such positions include:

Administrative Assistant
Office Manager
Office Services Specialist
Secretary
Staff Assistant
Word Processor

Here is a description of an office position supporting a college academic department:

OFFICE ASSISTANT

Duties:

> The Office Assistant will have the responsibility to coordinate student recruitment, retention, and graduation for the department's degree programs; answer inquiries relating to student recruitment and retention; maintain files, database, and mailing lists; collect application materials; and compile data and respond to surveys. In addition, he or she will coordinate and submit book orders, desk copy requests, student evaluations, submission of grades, materials for scholarship, awards, and internships; assist with the annual awards banquet or other departmental events; compose and type correspondence; update and maintain web pages; and process and route mail.

Minimum Qualifications:

> A high school diploma or GED and two years of related office experience, including word processing, are required.

Following are brief descriptions of three levels of Staff Assistant positions at Penn State University. As you can, each position classification (IV, V, or VI) has slightly different degrees of responsibility.

STAFF ASSISTANT IV, COLLEGE OF AGRICULTURAL SCIENCES

Duties:

The Staff Assistant IV will type correspondence, reports, forms, instructional and research materials, etc.; ensure that journal and proposal formats are followed; and file correspondence, reports, forms, and instructional, research, and extension materials. The person in this position also will answer telephones, greet visitors, provide information, or refer; schedule appointments; open, sort, and distribute mail; process outgoing and incoming mail; and monitor and maintain building office supply inventory.

Qualifications:

This position requires additional specialized training beyond the high school level or the completion of a formal high school vocational program or equivalent, plus three months of work-related experience. Computer experience and good typing (50 words or more with 5 or fewer errors) are preferred.

STAFF ASSISTANT V, COLLEGE OF SCIENCE
(ASSOCIATE DEAN'S OFFICE)

Duties:

The Staff Assistant V will process routine forms for Associate Dean's signature including University Faculty Senate petitions and monitor their progress; and process student forms and monitor their progress. This position serves as primary receptionist; answers telephones, greets visitors, provides information, and refers; covers office independently during lunch hour; monitors and collects forms from departments; ensures deadlines are met; and forwards paperwork to appropriate office for processing. In addition, the Staff Assistant V will update undergraduate students' records; assist in database management; schedule meeting rooms; work with departments and advising center for maintaining the database; arrange visits for prospective students and their families; maintain student files; maintain and update student lists for distribution to departments; process and sort incoming mail for three offices; read and answer incoming E-mail messages generated from online web site; copy, collate, and distribute information as needed; and maintain office supply inventory and purchase supplies.

Qualifications:

Additional specialized training beyond the high school level or completion of a formal high school vocational program or equivalent, plus three months of work-related experience are required. Experience with specific software packages appropriate to departmental needs is preferred.

STAFF ASSISTANT VI, COLLEGE OF ENGINEERING (DEPARTMENT OF ARCHITECTURAL ENGINEERING)

Duties:

The Staff Assistant VI will produce detailed yearly reports of utility use and cost for state agencies; collect data and verify the accuracy of utility usage for customers; work with customers to resolve discrepancies, interpret utility bills, and train individuals on how to properly complete monthly utility usage reports; maintain databases for office phone directory, coal reports, customer contacts, and vendors; and mail-merge word processing documents to produce labels and mailing lists. In addition, the person in this position will develop audiovisual presentations; coordinate conferences, seminars, and educational programs; assist in monitoring the educational programs of the institute and its customers; process forms and produce reports; process paperwork and time cards for occasional wage payroll employees; and answer phones, greet visitors, provide information or refer, schedule meetings, make travel arrangements, maintain office supplies and equipment, photocopy, open, sort, and distribute mail.

Qualifications:

Additional specialized training beyond the high school level or completion of a formal high school vocational program or equivalent, plus one year of work-related experience are required. Experience with appropriate software specific to departmental needs is preferred. Knowledge of spreadsheets and databases and word processing and math skills are also needed. Some travel is required.

Actual responsibilities for similar positions vary widely. In some cases, administrative support staff take a major role in handling complex duties within an office or department. In others, especially entry-level positions, they may handle a less complex range of duties such as word processing or serving as a receptionist.

INSTITUTIONAL RESEARCH

An area that may be somewhat obscure to the world outside of education is institutional research. But looking at this employment area may be revealing because it serves as an example of the importance of specialized support functions that may not be well known, but nevertheless provide significant support to the organization.

Institutional research involves studying various aspects of an institution's operations in a systematic way. Institutional researchers conduct grade studies, examine the effectiveness of instructional programs, complete analytical reports, and perform specialized research studies.

A typical day on the job may find the institutional researcher conducting research, analyses, and surveys to support planning and decision making; preparing statistical reports for internal use and external agencies; performing statistical computations and computer set-up tasks; coordinating the collection, analysis, processing, and reporting of data; providing data for evaluation of new programs and initiatives; providing data to support grant proposals; tracking graduate information; or coordinating or assisting in the institutional effectiveness process.

Following is a position description for an institutional research position at Cleveland State University.

DIRECTOR OF INSTITUTIONAL RESEARCH AND ANALYSIS

Job Duties:

> The Director of Institutional Research and Analysis provides leadership in the collection, analysis, interpretation, use, and dissemination of institutional data; coordinates and supervises the preparation of reports to meet the on-going data requirements of external agencies; provides data and information to senior managers in support of institutional planning and decision making; and undertakes special projects and ad hoc studies.
>
> Specific responsibilities include preparing routine internal and external data reports; ensuring compliance with all University, State, and Federal reporting require-

ments; coordinating the flow of key information among various units of the University; supervising preparation of a Fact Book; initiating and conducting studies on University policy implications and administrative issues; responding to internal and external requests for institutional data; monitoring state, regional, and national trends in higher education, especially in relation to urban institutions; and providing consultation on institutional research-related activities within the University.

Minimum Qualifications:

A master's degree in a related field and substantial experience in institutional research in a campus setting are required. A doctorate degree in a related field and substantial experience in institutional research in a campus setting are preferred. Ideally, the Director of Institutional Research and Analysis will be able to analyze, synthesize, and interpret statistical data; have strong presentation skills appropriate to a wide range of audiences; have experience with standard reports, research design, statistical tools and techniques, large databases, and use of the World Wide Web; possess strong leadership skills and some supervisory experience; and demonstrate excellent interpersonal and oral and written communication skills.

An entry-level position in the area of institutional research might have a title such as research assistant or research associate. Here is a description for such a position at Regents College in Albany, New York.

RESEARCH ASSOCIATE

Job Duties:

The Research Associate conducts studies on factors influencing success in distance education; participates in program-related studies such as outcomes assessment, curriculum review, and retention studies; develops and implements research across the college's academic divisions; analyzes complex data sets; develops surveys; prepares reports for technical and nontechnical audiences; and provides technical support to faculty and staff on data management issues.

Qualifications:

Minimum qualifications for this position include a Ph.D. in psychology, education, or a related discipline; advanced knowledge of statistics, research methods, survey development, and outcomes assessment; strong computer and communication skills; demonstrated ability to publish and present empirical research; and knowledge of appropriate software packages.

A similar position in a community college and some four-year schools would not require a doctorate, but other duties and requirements might be similar.

INSTRUCTIONAL DESIGN

An area of growing importance is instructional design. Work in this area involves developing academic courses or their components, or information and presentations to support them. For example, an instructional designer may work with a biology professor in developing an independent course in botany, helping create charts, graphs, photographic illustrations, and other information to be used in instructional modules.

Some instructional design personnel focus on specific technologies such as television or computers. Others provide specific functions such as writing scripts or creating photographs.

Here is an example of an instructional design position at Fort Hays State University in Kansas.

INSTRUCTIONAL DESIGNER

Duties:

> The duties of the Instructional Designer include working collaboratively with faculty members and media specialists to design and develop courses for distance and traditional environments; maintaining knowledge about emerging applications of instructional design theories and instructional technology applications; and participating in planning, preparing, and presenting workshops and instructional technology consulting services.

Qualifications:

> A master's degree and experience in course design and development, two years' experience designing instructional materials in higher education, and demonstrated knowledge of and experience with web-based, interactive television and video-based educational technologies are necessary.

HUMAN RESOURCES

Virtually every school district, college, or other educational organization maintains a human resources office. Once referred to as "personnel" but now more commonly known as "human resources," this function deals with hiring new personnel and providing support for existing employees in areas such as insurance and other fringe benefits.

Here is an example of an Assistant Vice President position in this area at the University of Rhode Island.

ASSISTANT VICE PRESIDENT FOR HUMAN RESOURCES

Duties:

The Assistant Vice President for Human Resources will provide leadership and guidance for the Human Resources area of the University, and recommend, maintain, enforce, and suggest revisions of human resource policies and procedures to the Board of Governors and University.

He or she will oversee the administration of the Office of Human Resource Administration and the Office of Professional Development, Leadership and Organization Training, including employment and compensation services, recruitment, union relations, dispute resolution, employee communications and relations, development and training, employee benefits, and wage/salary administration.

The person in this position also will cultivate a work environment that encourages diversity, seeks opportunities for learning and growth for its employees, demonstrates respect and support, is service-oriented, fosters innovation and creativity, and utilizes progressive technology; take lead in developing policies and procedures designed to attract and retain an excellent and diverse workforce for a four-campus system; oversee planning, coordination, and management of university-wide human resource functions in accordance with State, Board of Governors, and University rules, regulations, and strategic goals; advise the President, Vice Presidents, and other University officials on human resource matters; and serve as the primary University representative concerning human resource matters with the Board of Governors and other State officials.

Requirements:

> A master's degree from an accredited university or college
> in human resources administration or a related field; ten
> years of progressively responsible experience in human re-
> sources administration in the public or private sector, with
> specific experience in compensation and benefits pro-
> grams and experience in a union environment; experience
> in working effectively within a multicultural environment
> with a commitment to equal opportunity, diversity, and
> gender equity and a knowledge of successful strategies to
> recruit and retain a diverse workforce; and knowledge of
> complex human resource information systems technology
> in an Enterprise Resource Planning environment and its
> implementation are required.
>
> The Assistant Vice President for Human Resources
> must also possess excellent management, interpersonal,
> communication (both oral and written), and problem-
> solving skills combined with a collaborative leadership
> style; an ability to create and lead a forward-thinking,
> service-oriented human resource organization; demon-
> strated competence in leading major organizational
> change; a commitment to foster an organization that sup-
> ports and serves the University's teaching, research, and
> service missions; and a commitment to create a work cul-
> ture that emphasizes continuous improvement in its sys-
> tems and services, and training and development for its
> employees.

As can be seen from this description, working in human resources requires specialized knowledge. People holding management roles in this area usually have earned a bachelor's or master's
degree in human resources, personnel administration, business administration, or a related area, and have had substantial course
work or experience in the field. Support positions providing cleri-

cal functions also are included in this area, and may represent entry-level employment possibilities.

COMPUTER SUPPORT

One of the hottest employment areas in education, just as in the private sector, is the area of computer support. This includes a wide range of positions including programmer/analysts, computer technicians, directors of computer services, and other positions.

With the explosive growth of the Internet, positions in web-design and web-page management also play important roles in many educational institutions. At Westminster College in Utah, the position of Web Designer serves the college in a number of ways.

WEB DESIGNER

Duties:

> The Web Designer is responsible for designing, develop-ing, implementing, and maintaining the college's Intranet site; overseeing site and content creation; performing user account creation, moderating user rights, and resolv-ing web-related technology needs and problems; working with the web team on overall site development, including advising and directing departments and individuals in us-ing the website with respect to site creation, mainte-nance, style, tools, and upkeep; and developing client-side web pages, server-side technologies, and web soft-ware training for the college community.

Qualifications:

> A bachelor's degree in communications, media, or a related field; experience with website and multimedia

production; and at least two years of relevant experience in an academic setting are required.

Examples of other computer support positions include:

Chief Information Officer
Database Administrator
Help Desk Coordinator
Information Systems Coordinator
Network Services Technician
Programmer Analyst
Senior Programmer

The overall area of computer support holds great potential. Educational institutions rely increasingly on their computer infrastructures. Personnel who install and maintain computer equipment and provide related services play important roles, and this area offers solid career potential.

FACILITIES MANAGERS AND STAFF

Another specialized area involves planning, constructing, and maintaining the buildings that make up college campuses or school districts. These facilities management roles include:

Associate Director, Physical Plant
Director of Facilities Management
Director of Physical Plant
Physical Plant Manager
Plant and Utilities Engineer

Here is an example of a position that focuses on the planning of educational buildings.

FACILITIES PLANNER

Duties:

The Facilities Planner prepares planning studies and conducts analyses, develops documents defining program requirements, forecasts plant capacity and utilization, conducts research and makes recommendations, relates aspects of architecture, coordinates committees and outside consultant activities and planning projects, assists in the development and maintenance of computer systems, and assists in the review of construction documents.

Minimum Qualifications:

Basic requirements for this position include a bachelor's degree in architecture, interior architecture, planning, or a related field; and four years of experience in writing and editing program planning documents. Experience in developing and analyzing cost/budget data in support of capital projects; applying physical and space standards or guidelines; and translating program activities into physical space requirements is necessary, as are a knowledge of facility planning and university/institution processes and a record of progressively responsible work experience in facility planning or equivalent.

Other related jobs involve the day-to-day management of physical facilities. Here is description for such a position at Kansas-based Fort Hays State University:

DIRECTOR OF THE PHYSICAL PLANT

Duties:

The Director of the Physical Plant has responsibility for the day-to-day operations and fiscal and personnel management of the following campus units: custodial services, grounds, building maintenance, construction, environmental safety, power plant, mechanical and electrical infrastructure maintenance, motor pool, warehouse/shipping and receiving, printing services, the mailroom, and emergency preparedness.

Specific responsibilities in addition to the fiscal, personnel, and day-to-day management include:

- Working closely with the Vice President for Administration and Finance to establish, approve, and implement operating procedures to secure and protect the assets and personnel of the institution, including assurance of safe working places, control of parking, traffic, and emergency procedures;
- Managing the buildings, grounds, and infrastructure of the university and establishing, approving, and implementing operating procedures to utilize, control, and account for these assets;
- Advising University Police and the Vice President for Administration and Finance in matters relating to campus security;
- Establishing, approving, and implementing procedures to ensure compliance with all laws, regulations, and codes regarding fire safety, hazardous waste, asbestos, and other areas of regulatory and legal concern;
- Working closely with the Director of Facilities Planning to maximize resources available for facilities maintenance and enhancement;
- In conjunction with University Police, establishing, approving, implementing, and maintaining an emergency preparedness plan for the University and working closely with city, county, and state officials in its application;

- Implementing and administering energy management procedures and plans to include the procurement of fuel oil, electricity, and natural gas and the deployment and management of energy conservation systems;
- Establishing, approving, and implementing operating procedures to provide centralized support services for campus mail, printing services, the motor pool, and the warehouse;
- Maintaining harmonious relationships with faculty, staff, students, external entities, and the public;
- Maintaining cooperative working relationships with the Department of Student Residential Life, the Memorial Union, and the University Farm;
- Developing appropriate systems to enhance campus-wide physical plant operations and to continually assess their effectiveness by measuring customer satisfaction and other indicators consistent with the University's continuous improvement efforts; and
- Recommending to the Vice President for Administration and Finance opportunities for university-wide improvement.

Education:

The Director of the Physical Plant should have a bachelor's degree, preferably in an engineering or technical discipline. Substantial managerial experience (ten or more years, five of which must be in a higher education setting) managing one or more of the operational areas for which the Director is responsible can substitute for the degree requirement.

Experience:

The Director of the Physical Plant must have five or more years of experience managing one or more of the operational areas for which the Director is responsible. Experience must include supervision of ten or more positions and carry responsibility for a minimum annual nonpersonnel budget of $10,000.

TRANSPORTATION

Some jobs involve transporting students. One of the most common is that of a school bus driver. This position does not require additional education or degrees beyond a high school diploma. Here is a brief description of requirements for a school bus driver's position in Wyoming:

SCHOOL BUS DRIVER

Job Description:

The School Bus Driver operates motor vehicles to transport passengers and provide a safe atmosphere.

Requirements:

The person in this position must have a good driving record, be at least eighteen years of age, and pass a physical examination.

Training:

Most employers provide new employees with on-the-job training.

License:

All school bus drivers must have a commercial driver's license.

Other related positions include those of transportation coordinator and director or assistant director of transportation. These positions may require additional training, education, and job experience.

CHAPTER 7

EDUCATIONAL PREPARATION

A key to most careers in educational support areas is obtaining the right educational credentials. In some jobs, like those in basic support areas such as facilities services or clerical assistance, a high school diploma and on-the-job training may suffice. But for many positions, a bachelor's, master's, or even a doctoral degree may be expected, depending on the level and type of position involved.

Exact educational requirements vary widely, as do the options for obtaining appropriate credentials. In addition to degree requirements, some positions (such as those of principals and assistant principals) require special certification.

In this chapter, a variety of educational options are profiled.

EDUCATIONAL ADMINISTRATION

In educational administration, an advanced degree is a common requirement. Many colleges and universities offer training in educational administration, educational leadership, or related areas.

For example, the Department of Educational Administration at the University of Nebraska offers programs for persons pursuing careers as administrators in a variety of roles. Students completing a master's degree program may earn either a Master of Arts (M.A.) or a Master of Education (M.Ed.) degree with a major in educational administration. Many students who study in these areas also meet the requirements for a Nebraska Administrative and Supervisory Certificate to become eligible for employment for administrative positions in the public schools.

Students may pursue any of the following three areas:

1. Background in the organization and operation of schools, with initial endorsements in administration provided in the areas of supervisor of special education, supervisor of speech pathology and audiology, elementary principal, middle-level principal, secondary principal, and curriculum supervisor.

2. Specialization in athletics, student affairs, or administration positions in higher education, with endorsements provided in the areas of specialization in supervision of 7–12 activities, administration of postsecondary athletics, student affairs in postsecondary institutions, and administration positions in higher education.

3. Foundation of study and research to prepare for specialization as a researcher and scholar in a general area of educational administration.

For more information contact:

The Department of Educational Administration
University of Nebraska-Lincoln
1204 Seaton Hall
Lincoln, NE 68588-0638

At Michigan State University, students may earn a master of arts degree focusing on K–12 administration. The program includes the following four component areas:

Area 1. Consists of two required courses: Organizational Theory in Education, and Approaches to Educational Research. These courses provide an introduction to the major themes of the program, including an understanding of schools as organizations and an exploration of contemporary approaches to inquiry.

Area 2. Students select from a group of courses on educational leadership functions. If you pursue a degree in this area, you might take courses such as Leadership and Organizational Development; Planning, Budgeting, and Evaluation; Administration of Human Resources in Education; Elementary and Middle School Administration; Secondary School Administration; Legal, Fiscal, and Policy Environment of Schools; Schools, Families, and Communities; and Instructional Supervision.

Area 3. Provides an opportunity to take one to two elective courses outside the department.

Area 4. Students complete a capstone experience in which they design and conduct a field-based, applied research project on an educational question or problem.

For more information contact:

College of Education
   Michigan State University
   134 Erickson Hall
   East Lansing, MI 48824

A college or university near you may offer a range of degrees in the field of education. Appalachian State University in North Carolina, for example, offers a number of programs in this area, including Master's in School Administration, Master of Arts in Higher Education—Developmental Education, Master of Arts in

Higher Education—Teaching, Master of Arts in Higher Education—Adult Education, Master of Arts—Instructional Technology Specialist—Computers, Master of Arts in Higher Education—Administration, Educational Specialist—Public School Administration, Educational Specialist—Higher Education Administration, Educational Specialist—Higher Education—Adult Education, Educational Specialist—Higher Education—Developmental Education, and Educational Specialist—Media (for librarians).

A typical program of study is that required for the Master's in School Administration (M.S.A.) degree. To be admitted, students must have a bachelor's degree from an accredited college or university, acceptable Graduate Record Exam or Miller Analogy Test scores, approval of the admissions committees or the chairperson of the department, and an appropriate teaching certification.

To earn the master's, students complete forty-two semester hours in areas such as research in education, social and philosophical foundations of education, applied organizational theory, educational leadership, curriculum planning, critical inquiry and thought in educational leadership, studies in applied instruction, plus electives.

More details about this and other programs in educational administration are available by contacting:

Appalachian State University
  Boone, NC 28608

COUNSELING PROGRAMS

Counseling is another area where an advanced degree is commonly required. Many universities offer master's- or doctoral-level programs in counseling.

For instance, Indiana University offers a master's degree program in counseling and counselor education. This is a forty-eight credit-hour program requiring at least two years of study. The program allows students to chose from a school track or a community track. Students preparing for careers in counseling may enroll in a variety of courses, some of which are required and some which are electives, depending on program direction. Here are descriptions for some (not all) of the courses available in this area.

Professional Orientation and Ethics

Studies that provide an understanding of all aspects of professional functioning including history, roles, organizational structures, ethics, standards, and credentialing.

Individual Appraisal: Principles and Procedures

An analysis of statistical, psychometric, sociometric, and clinical principles crucial to professional interpretation of standardized and informal data regarding individual clients. Current issues/controversies about ethnic, sex, cultural, and individual differences will be examined.

Counseling Theory

Introduction to counseling theories and psychological processes involved in individual counseling.

Laboratory in Counseling

Laboratory experiences in counseling, analysis of counseling interviews, role playing, and closely supervised counseling in the laboratory setting.

School Counseling: Intervention, Consultation, and Program Development

Foundations and contextual dimensions of school counseling. Knowledge and skills for the practice of school counseling. Developmental counseling. Program development, implementation, and evaluation. Consultation. Principles, practices, and applications of needs assessment. Provides an overall understanding of the organization of schools and the function of the counselor and the counseling program.

An Introduction to Values Clarification Techniques

A theoretical and practical basis for values clarification in human assessment and development. The psychology of valuing. Values clarification in human adjustment, problem-solving, decision making, and self-understanding. Values clarification techniques for counselors, helping professionals, teachers, and other educators.

Communication Skills and Interpersonal Relations in Counseling

A study of basic skills of interviewing: attending, encouragement to talk, paraphrasing, summarization of content, responding to feeling and summarization of feeling, when to use skills, situations in which different communication skills may be used.

Seminar in Career Development: Theory and Research

Examination of psychological basis and theoretical approaches to vocational development; review of research relevant to career development and career counseling.

For more information about Indiana University's counseling programs, contact:

Indiana University, Bloomington
  School of Education
  Counseling Programs
  Bloomington, IN 47405

At Emporia State University in Kansas, students may prepare for certification as counselors working in elementary, middle, or secondary school. Students in this master's-level program compete forty-eight total hours as follows.

Core Courses:

Multicultural Counseling
Professional and Ethical Issues in Counseling Pre-Practicum
Counseling Skills Development, Individual and Group Appraisal
Career Counseling and Development
Counseling Theories
Theories of Group Counseling
Psychosocial Development and Disability

Concentration:

Introduction to Secondary School Counseling
Introduction to Elementary/Middle School Counseling
Parenting and Parent Consultation
Management of Counseling Programs

Research:

Research Design and Writing (nonthesis option), or
Research Design and Writing (thesis option)

A practicum and internship also are required, and electives may be completed if the nonthesis option is selected.

For more details contact:

Counselor Education and Rehabilitation Programs
Campus Box 4036
Emporia State University
Emporia, KS 66801

LIBRARY AND INFORMATION STUDIES

Some positions in educational libraries, such those of library assistants or other paraprofessionals, do not require completion of a specific degree. But for jobs as professional librarians, a master's degree is a common requirement. Many colleges and universities in the United States and Canada offer programs in library studies, which may be called by any number of names.

McGill University in Montreal offers a typical selection of courses in this area. Here are some examples of course descriptions in McGill's master's degree program in library and information studies:

Organization of Information (3 credits)

>   Theory and techniques of bibliographic control for information. Basic cataloging and indexing principles and practices incorporating the concepts of main entry, subject analysis, and classification according to standard codes. Introduction to ISBD and MARC formats for description and automated support applications. Practical assignments in the organization of materials laboratory.

Classification and Cataloging (3 credits)

>   Cataloging in depth with a view to such specialties as original cataloging, catalog maintenance, and administration of the cataloging department. Investigation of alternative methods of library documentation. Developments in international cataloging standards, codes, and formats. Includes laboratory sessions.

Research Principles and Analysis (3 credits)

>   Fundamental aspects of reflective thinking and the methods and techniques of research appropriate to the investigation of library/information problems. Criteria helpful in evaluating published research in library/information studies by analyzing the various steps of the research process, thereby providing guidelines for planning, conducting, and reporting research.

History of Books and Printing (3 credits)

>   Surveyed are the development of writing, alphabets, and books from their inception, and of printing from its in-

vention in the fifteenth century. Historical bibliography dealing with the various physical elements in book production, including design.

Public Libraries (3 credits)

A review of the Public Library Movement in English and French Canada. The development of public libraries in North America over the last twenty years with an emphasis on the library's role and responsibilities for the future. The impact of information technologies on the definition and delivery of services.

Bibliographic and Factual Sources (3 credits)

Introduces students to the theory, principles, and practice of bibliographical control as a foundation for reference service and information retrieval. Paper-based, microform, and electronic bibliographies are introduced. The creation and use of bibliographies, within various contexts, are discussed.

Online Information Retrieval (3 credits)

Focuses on the principles and methods of information retrieval from full-text and bibliographic databases. Includes information-seeking behavior, database organizations and characteristics, search and browsing strategies, and search and system evaluation, as applied to online databases, CD-ROMS, OPACS, and Internet resources.

Marketing Information Services (3 credits)

The role and use of marketing for information brokers and library or information centers are discussed. Various aspects of the marketing process as applied to information services are analyzed. Students prepare a preliminary marketing plan for an information service of their choice and share similarities and differences in these specific applications.

Multimedia Systems (3 credits)

> Theoretical and applied principles of multimedia system design. Includes knowledge representation; interfaces; storage and retrieval of text, sound, still images, animation and video sequences; authoring software; hardware options; CD-ROM/DVD and web-based systems; virtual reality; testing and evaluation. Students design and develop a small-scale system.

Descriptive Bibliography (3 credits)

> A practical course on the history, description, and care of rare books and antiquarian material. The principles of descriptive bibliography will be presented in the context of book culture. The place of rare book collections in research libraries and the practical administration of a rare book department will be examined.

For more information about these and other courses, contact:

McGill University
  459 McTavish Street
  Montreal, Quebec
  Canada H3A 1Y1

Media Specialist

In some programs, a minor or specialization is available in the area of media studies. At the University of Northern Iowa, students may complete a library media specialist minor by completing the following courses along with courses required for the major:

  Educational Television Production
  Organization of Information

Introduction to School Library Media Program
Library Resources for Children or Library Resources for Young
   Adults
School Library Media Curriculum Development
Administration of the School Library Media Program
Reference Services and Information Retrieval
Practicum

The minor requirements total twenty-four credit hours. Students
who complete this program are eligible for either a K–6 or grade
7–12 media specialist endorsement, depending on the level of basic teaching license.

More details are available by contacting:

College of Education
   University of Northern Iowa
   Cedar Falls, IA 50614

INSTITUTIONAL RESEARCH

In some areas, such as institutional research, a specific degree is
not required or expected. Instead, a background in math, statistics,
or another analytical area will suffice. This may be supplemented
by specialized training such as short-term courses or seminars.

For those interested in the field of institutional research, the Association for Institutional Research (AIR) offers various conferences and workshops. In addition, AIR offers summer institutes in
the areas of enrollment management, foundations for the practice
of institutional research, statistics, and technology.

AIR workshops, typically offered in conjunction with the association's annual forum, cover topics such as: "Using Market
Research in Higher Education," "Planning Today for Your Fiscal

Tomorrow," "Newcomer's Workshop for Professionals New to Institutional Research," "Research Design Ideas for Institutions," "Effective Internet Searches," "Intermediate Statistics for Institutional Research," "Basic Academic Resource Planning," "The Use of National Center for Education Statistics Databases for Institutional Research and Policy Analysis," "Qualitative Research Methods," and "Environmental Scanning."

Although these activities are designed for practicing institutional researchers, graduate students and others interested in breaking into the field may find them of interest. For more information contact:

The Association for Institutional Research
  114 Stone Building
  Tallahassee, FL 32306-4462

TEACHER'S AIDE

Some programs, often offered in community or technical colleges, focus on paraprofessional roles. For example, the teacher's aide program offered by Canada's Confederation College prepares students to work closely with education professionals in a school. The program develops skills in communications, microcomputers, psychology, and sociology. It includes core content to cover skills such as educational programming, arts and crafts, observation and record keeping, and computers in the classroom.

The program takes two years to complete, including both academic and practical applications. Academic courses allow students to become familiar with the development and needs of children, while practical applications build skills in creating learning centers, bulletin boards, games, and other activities. Field placements allow these techniques to be applied in the classroom where students receive feedback on their performance.

A typical sequence of courses in this program might look something like this:

First Semester

Course Number/Title		Credits
CS 101	Basic Communications	2.5
GE 122	Introduction to Crisis Support	3
HS 117	Windows for Service Professionals	2
TE 102	Library Techniques	3
TE 105	Role of the Educational Assistant	3
TE 106	The Arts in the School System	3
TE 110	Lifespan Development I	3
Total		19.5

Second Semester

Course Number/Title		Credits
CS 216	Intermediate Communications	2.5
TE 202	Educational Programming	4
TE 206	Practicum I	4
TE 208	Student Exceptionalities I	3
TE 220	Lifespan Development II	3
General Education Elective		3
Total		19.5

Third Semester

Course Number/Title		Credits
TE 302	Observation and Record Keeping	3
TE 305	Student Exceptionalities II	3
TE 309	Child Abuse	2.5
TE 311	Computers in the Classroom	3
TE 312	Adolescent Development	3
TE 313	Basic Pharmacology	3
Total		17.5

Fourth Semester

Course Number/Title		Credits
GE 520	Success in the New Economy	1
TE 405	Placement Review	2
TE 414	Practicum II	24
Total		27

For more information contact:

Confederation College
P.O. Box 398
Thunder Bay, Ontario
Canada P7C 4W1

Pennsylvania's Montgomery County Community College offers another program to train teacher's aides. This program helps students become familiar with the range of responsibilities that a teacher's aide has and prepares them for employment in both public and private schools.

A typical program of study will include courses such as these:

First Semester

English Composition
Introduction to Psychology
Keyboarding
Introduction to Education
Introduction to Sociology

Second Semester

English Composition II
Child Psychology
Science Elective
Elective (education)
Marriage and the Family

Third Semester

Introduction to Speech Communication
Educational Psychology
Teaching Young Children to Read
Safety and First Aid
Introduction to Educational Media
Movement Experiences and Games in Elementary Education

Fourth Semester

Literature in Early Childhood and Elementary Education
Observation and Participation in Elementary School
Teaching of Science in Preschool and Elementary Grades
Elective (education)

For more information contact:

Montgomery County Community College
340 DeKalb Pike
Blue Bell, PA 19422

CERTIFICATION

Certification usually involves either completing a specific educational program, passing one or more special exams, or both. In some cases, certification is required to hold a given position (such as that of a principal). In others (such as certification for secretaries or administrative assistants), it is optional but stands as an indicator of competency.

Most states have specific requirements for eligibility to hold administrative positions in public schools. For example, the state of Florida requires the following for any person who holds an administrative position.

- Completion of courses in eight domains of educational administration/leadership:

  1. Public School Curriculum and Instruction
  2. Organizational Management and Development
  3. Human Resource Management and Development
  4. Leadership Skills
  5. Communication Skills
  6. Technology
  7. Educational Law
  8. Educational Finance

- Verification of three years of successful teaching experience in an elementary or secondary school.
- Possession of a valid regular teaching certificate for the state of Florida.

- Documentation of successful completion of a Beginning Teacher Program or possession of a continuing or professional services contract or tenure.
- Possession of a master's or higher degree awarded by an appropriate institution as defined by state rules.
- Documentation of successful completion of at least six semester hours of graduate credit, or the equivalent, in specified academic areas such as early childhood/primary education or secondary school education.
- A passing score for Level I Certification in the state of Florida.

Secretaries and other administrative personnel may want to pursue the CPS (certified professional secretary) rating offered by the International Association of Administrative Professionals (IAAP). This certification demonstrates to employers and others that certain skill levels have been attained. This can be helpful both in applying for jobs in schools and colleges (as well as with other employers) and in advancing on the job. IAAP studies have shown that those holding CPS certification earn average salaries that are significantly higher than those without this certification. In addition, many colleges and universities offer credit for preparing for and passing the CPS exam.

The CPS examination is a one-day exam, administered twice yearly, at more than 250 locations across the United States, Canada, and other countries. It covers three major areas: finance and business law (including economics, accounting, and business law); office systems and administration (covering office technology, office administration, and business communication); and management (including behavioral science in business, human resources management, and organizations and management).

An *Examination Review Guide* that contains the examination outline, a bibliography, sample questions, and other helpful information is available from the association. Colleges and IAAP chapters also offer CPS review courses to assist in exam preparation.

For more information contact:

International Association
    of Administrative Professionals
10502 NW Ambassador Drive
P.O. Box 20404
Kansas City, MO 64195-0404

PLANNING YOUR EDUCATION

For most people, there are many steps involved in pursuing an educational support career. Typically, such steps include checking out the programs offered by various colleges and universities to be sure you are choosing the right college. Next you will need to apply for financial aid or otherwise obtain the necessary financial resources so that you can complete the college program in your desired area. Depending on your interest, you will complete an appropriate graduate program and take on as much as you can in terms of work experience, internships, part-time or summer employment, or other experiences. Finally, you will go on for certification, if you need to.

SELECTING A COLLEGE

In choosing a college, consider the following questions, as suggested by the U.S. Department of Education: Does the school offer the courses and type of program I want? Do I meet the admissions requirements? Does the school offer a quality education at a reasonable price? Does the school offer services I need and activities in which I'm interested?

Most of this information is covered in any college's catalog or in its introductory brochures, and in many cases, via the Internet, since many colleges and universities have websites. To obtain a list of schools on the Internet, one good place to look is at the IPEDS COOL Institution List at www.nces.ed.gov/ipeds/cool/InstList.asp.

Other factors to consider when choosing a college include the opinions of friends or relatives who have previously attended the school; evidence that the college is fully accredited; the school's loan default rate (that is, the percentage of students who attended the school, took out federal student loans, and later failed to repay their loans on time); campus security policies and campus crime statistics; job placement rates; the school's refund policy; completion and transfer rates; and availability of financial aid.

When seriously considering any college, visit the campus at least once to get a firsthand look. At the same time, don't forget that choosing a college is not necessarily a permanent decision. Keep in mind that you can always begin at one school and then transfer to another. But if you do your homework up front, you are less likely to waste time and money.

MEETING COLLEGE EXPENSES

While taking time to select a college, be sure to explore all the options for paying for your education. The cost of attending college is higher than ever and may include tuition, fees for a variety of purposes, book costs, computing costs, room and board, and travel or commuting expenses. The total may range from approximately $1,500 a year at a typical community college to more than $30,000 a year at some private colleges. Not surprisingly, most students will want to pursue some type of financial assistance.

Virtually all colleges and universities offer some combination of scholarships, grants, loans, and other types of aid, and thousands of private organizations offer scholarships or other assistance. State-level aid also is widely available.

The federal government offers a number of student aid options. For example, there are Pell Grants, which are offered as outright grants; in other words, these awards do not have to be repaid. They may be are awarded to undergraduate students who have not earned bachelors' or professional degrees. Pell Grants are based on financial need, with the neediest students obtaining the largest awards.

FSEOG, or Federal Supplemental Educational Opportunity Grants, are intended for undergraduates with exceptional financial need. Pell Grant recipients with extra financial need also may receive FSEOG awards.

The Federal Work-Study program provides part-time jobs for undergraduate and graduate students who demonstrate financial need. Participating students receive wage-based financial assistance along with the opportunity to gain work experience while still in school.

Federal Perkins Loans may be received by undergraduate or graduate students with exceptional financial need. These loans must be repaid, but because of government backing, the interest rate is lower than most other types of loans.

Now offered through the William D. Ford Direct Loan Program, Stafford Loans are available to students who do not obtain sufficient help from other sources. Stafford Loans are available to students who do not necessarily have the level of need of students qualifying for other federal aid programs, but still have a need for financial assistance. Along with an interest rate that is lower than most commercial loans, they allow borrowers a long time (up to thirty years, if desired) for repayment.

The first step in applying for federal student aid is to complete a Free Application for Federal Student Aid (FAFSA). This can be done online, or you may submit a written application in English or Spanish.

For more information, consult the U.S. Department of Education home page at www.fafsa.ed.gov or write to:

Federal Student Aid Information Center
  P.O. Box 84
  Washington, DC 20044
  1-800/4-FED-AID (1-800/433-3243)

Also, be sure to check out the many other types of aid available, including scholarships offered by colleges or various other organizations, state-sponsored grants and scholarships, and other sources of scholarships, loans or other aid. You can identify funding sources by consulting the U.S. Department of Education home page and other websites about financial aid and scholarships, checking with college financial aid offices and high school guidance counselors, or looking through financial aid directories available in bookstores and libraries.

CHAPTER 8

SALARIES AND BENEFITS

A major incentive in any job is salary. Even though people who work in education often are motivated by the desire to serve others, the ability to earn a good salary is also important.

Salaries and wages earned in educational support careers vary widely. A frequent criticism is that those working in education are underpaid. Although a case can certainly be made for this point of view, many positions pay attractive salaries and offer excellent fringe benefits.

Salaries may vary due to a variety of factors. In a small, rural school district or college, salaries may be much lower than those earned by staff employed in urban areas, at state universities, or at prestigious private schools. In a state department of education or national organization, salary levels may be highly competitive. For technical specialists or administrators with substantial management responsibilities, excellent salaries are possible.

Of course in general terms, salaries paid by educational institutions or related organizations are not as high as those for comparable positions in private business. Because schools typically rely on government funding or private donations, they tend to avoid paying extremely high salaries as a matter of both practicality and image. Not only do budget realities limit salaries, but it is often necessary to keep salaries at a moderate level in keeping with the institution's public service image. Normally, benefits such as stock options and profit-sharing plans are not available in the educational sector.

Nevertheless, salaries in educational support jobs can be attractive. In addition, many employers offer liberal fringe benefits.

POTENTIAL SALARY LEVELS

According to the U.S. Department of Labor, 1997 median hourly wages in several categories were as follows for those working in educational services:

Educational administrators	$29.12
Secretaries	$10.76
General office clerks	$ 9.10
Teacher's aides	$ 7.51

On an yearly basis, this equates to an average salary of more than $60,000 for administrative personnel. At the very top of the scale, college presidents and school superintendents often earn between $100,000 and $200,000, and some earn substantially more. For mid-level managers, however, salaries ranging from $35,000 to $70,000 yearly are more common.

Counselors in elementary and secondary schools had median incomes of slightly more than $42,000 in 1997, while those in colleges and universities averaged $34,700 (a lower figure, in part, because a greater variety of positions in colleges lowers the average for all positions). Librarians at both levels averaged slightly more than $38,000 annually.

For clerical personnel and other support staff, salaries of $20,000 to $30,000 are common. Some lower-level positions pay less than $20,000 yearly, and bus drivers or aides who may not work full-time may earn substantially less.

Factors Influencing Salary Levels

Not surprisingly, schools located in affluent areas or colleges with a strong funding base are most likely to pay the best salaries. Other factors influencing salary levels may include credentials and educational background. In educational institutions, it is common for personnel who have earned master's or doctoral degrees to earn higher salaries than those with a bachelor's as their highest degree, other factors being roughly equal. For staff support jobs, those with an associate or bachelor's degree may earn higher pay than those with only a high school diploma. Although salaries are not always tied directly to educational background, many school districts, colleges, and other educational organizations maintain salary schedules that include educational level as a major factor in determining salary level.

Previous experience also plays a part in determining one's salary. In general, employees with substantial experience tend to earn higher salaries. Both for long-time employees within a given institution and for those who move from one school or organization to another, more experienced personnel normally command higher salaries than those who are less experienced.

Geographical location is another factor in establishing wage and salary levels. People who work in large cities or other areas with a relatively high cost of living usually earn more than employees holding similar positions in more rural areas. For instance, community college administrators working in San Francisco or Houston tend to earn more than those employed in Mobile, Alabama, or Omaha, Nebraska.

The type of employer also plays a role in how much you can expect to make. Typically, a major administrator at a large university will earn more than an administrator at a small community college. A church-run kindergarten will probably pay lower salaries than a public school in the same area. Depending on the type of employer, salaries for similar positions may vary substantially.

Overall economic conditions may affect salary levels. Full-time employees often receive yearly raises that take inflation into account along with other factors.

Typically, the more responsibility a job involves, the higher the salary level. Positions involving management of other employees, in particular, often pay at a higher level due to the supervisory responsibilities involved.

FRINGE BENEFITS

Along with salaries, most schools or other educational employers provide a variety of benefits to employees. Such benefits can be a significant plus and in some cases, can help offset modest pay scales.

Employees in schools, colleges, and related organizations usually earn some combination of the following benefits: paid holidays and vacation time; health, dental, life, and disability insurance; sick and personal time; retirement plans; retiree and death benefits; tuition assistance; and scholarships for children of employees.

All employers do not offer all of these benefits, so it is a good idea to review and compare benefits when considering potential employment situations.

Also, keep in mind that some benefits are paid in their entirety by the employer; for others, employees contribute part of the cost.

At the University of Washington, for example, benefits include medical, dental, and lifelong term disability; retirement and voluntary investment programs; a "Hometown Home Loan Program" providing employees with discounts on loan fees, inspections, and appraisal fees; Dependent Care Assistance Program (DCAP); auto, home, renter, and boat insurance; and paid vacation days, sick leave, and holidays. Other benefits include tuition exemption, computer training classes, and recreational sports.

Young people just beginning their careers might be especially interested in educational assistance. Such benefits might consist of tuition reimbursement (where the employer reimburses the cost of college courses completed successfully by the employee), direct payment of tuition, tuition wavers (offered by colleges and universities for their own employees), or other support of educational endeavors. Some schools or other educational employers will even provide paid time off to attend classes or unpaid leave on an extended basis without the need to give up a position.

CHAPTER 9

PROFESSIONAL ASSOCIATIONS

Participating in a professional organization can be of significant benefit. Such groups link together people with common career or professional interests. Although of primary benefit to those employed in a given area, they also can be of interest to students and others seeking information or assistance.

Professional associations may consist of hundreds or thousands of voluntary members who join together to share information, promote their profession, and work toward common goals. Usually, officers are elected from the membership on an annual basis. Larger associations often employ paid staff to coordinate the group activities. The combination of volunteer and staff resources typically provides a wide range of services to members.

BENEFITS OF PARTICIPATING
IN PROFESSIONAL ASSOCIATIONS

There are many reasons for participating in professional associations. For example, you will have the chance to network with others who work in the same field or a related area, the opportunity to learn from experienced professionals or colleagues with knowledge and experience in selected areas, and the opportunity to participate in professional meetings (conferences, workshops, or conventions) sponsored by the association. Memberships in professional associations also provide a convenient way to keep up with new developments through journals, newsletters, or other publications; and the chance to acquire new knowledge through classes, seminars, or other professional development activities.

REPRESENTATIVE PROFESSIONAL ASSOCIATIONS

Following is an overview of just some of the professional associations serving those who work in educational support areas. To identify additional such groups, check with current employees in the area in which you're interested.

American Association of Collegiate Registrars and Admissions Officers

More than 9,000 members belong to the American Association of Collegiate Registrars and Admissions Officers (AACRAO). Members represent nearly 2,500 colleges and other agencies and institutions in the United States and in twenty-eight countries around the world.

This association focuses on identifying and promoting standards and best practices in enrollment management, information technology, instructional management, and student services.

For more information contact the organization at the following address:

American Association of Collegiate Registrars
    and Admissions Officers
One Dupont Circle NW, Suite 520
Washington, DC 20036
www. aacrao.org

American Association of School Administrators

Founded in 1865, the American Association of School Administrators (AASA) serves more than 14,000 educational leaders in the United States, Canada, and other organizations. It has four major focus areas: improving the condition of children and youth, preparing schools and school systems for the twenty-first century, connecting schools and communities, and enhancing the quality and effectiveness of school leaders.

The association focuses on elementary and secondary education and provides a variety of services.

For more details contact:

American Association of School Administrators
1801 North Moore Street
Arlington, VA 22209
www.aasa.org

American College Personnel Association

The American College Personnel Association (ACPA) serves student affairs professionals in colleges and universities. A major objective is fostering professional development through annual conventions, teleconferences, regional workshops, and specialty conferences. The association also supports professional networking, provides placement services, and provides personal benefits such as liability insurance.

ACPA publications include the *Journal of College Student Development,* published six times per year; *About Campus: Enriching the Student Learning Experience,* another bimonthly publication; books on topics of interest to student affairs educators; quarterly newsletters; a *Member Resource Directory*; and other publications of various types. Of special interest to students is a directory of graduate programs in the field.

More details about the association and its services may be obtained from:

American College Personnel Association
One Dupont Circle, Suite 300
Washington, DC 20036

American School Counselor Association

The ASCA has a membership of more than 12,000 school counseling professionals. Founded in 1952, it focuses on professional development, enhancement of school counseling programs, and research on effective school counseling. It serves school counselors in public and private prekindergarten; elementary, middle, and junior high schools; and secondary and postsecondary schools.

The association publishes a journal, *Professional School Counseling,* and a newspaper, the *ASCA Counselor.* It also provides a number of other services for members.

More details are available by contacting:

American School Counselor Association
801 North Fairfax Street, Suite 310
Alexandria, VA 22314

Association for the Advancement of Computing in Education

AACE, founded in 1981, promotes the advancement of the knowledge, theory, and quality of learning and teaching at all levels with information technology.

The major purposes of the association are encouraging scholarly inquiry related to information technology in education and disseminating research results and their applications. This is done through publications, conferences, meetings, and projects conducted in cooperation with other organizations.

More information about AACE is available from:

Association for the Advancement of Computing in Education
Box 2966
Charlottesville, VA 22902

Association for Educational Communications and Technology

The AECT provides leadership in educational communications and technology. It links professionals holding a common interest in the use of educational technology and its application to the learning process. It serves professionals in the audiovisual media, library, and microcomputing; education administrators; and others involved in the use of instructional technology.

Services and activities offered by this organization include an annual convention as well as regional and national seminars focusing on leadership and professional development; divisional activities offered through the association's eleven divisions; publications including "Tech Trends," *Educational Technology Research & Development* and *Quarterly Review of Distance Education;* and job placement services.

For more information about these and other services, contact the organization at:

Association for Educational Communications and Technology
1800 North Stonelake Drive
Bloomington, IN 47404

Association for Institutional Research

The Association for Institutional Research (AIR) is a professional organization for those involved in higher education who have a strong interest in management research, policy analysis, and planning. Members work in a variety of postsecondary areas including finance, academic affairs, instruction, student services, and institutional development.

Services provided by AIR include an annual forum featuring hundreds of papers and panel presentations; professional development opportunities in the form of workshops, institutes, grants, and scholarships; and publications including books, journals, and newsletters.

For more information on AIR publications and services, contact:

Association for Institutional Research
  Executive Office
  114 Stone Building
  Florida State University
  Tallahassee, FL 32306-4462

Association for Supervision and Curriculum Development

The Association for Supervision and Curriculum Development (ASCD) is a nonpartisan association of professional educators from diverse backgrounds. Formed in 1943, the organization promotes advancements in teaching and learning.

ASCD takes positions on issues of importance to educators and provides a forum in education issues and professionalism. It offers conferences and meetings on emerging issues and professional training opportunities for educators. The association also has several publications including *Educational Leadership,* the *Journal of Curriculum and Supervision,* and *Education Update.*

For more information contact:

Association for Supervision and Curriculum Development
  1703 North Beauregard Street
  Alexandria, VA 22311-1714

Canadian Association of Principals

The Canadian Association of Principals (CAP) represents principals and vice principals of schools. It is made up of associations from each province.

Canadian Association of Principals services and programs include professional development activities such as national and regional workshops and an annual conference, a journal and newsletter, an online discussion service, special projects conducted in partnership with other organizations and government departments, and information of interest to educators.

Additional details about the association are available from:

Canadian Association of Principals
  2835 Country Woods Drive
  Surrey, British Columbia V4P 9P9

Canadian Council of Montessori Administrators

This not-for-profit corporation was founded in 1977 to support Montessori school administrators in Canada. It offers knowledge and expertise in Montessori school administration and the Montessori method of education.

The council sponsors workshops, conferences, meetings, public awareness initiatives, and a newsletter. It also provides evaluation services to assist members in developing and maintaining high standards.

More information about the council is available by contacting:

Canadian Council of Montessori Administrators
  Box 54534
  Toronto, Ontario M5M 4N5
  www.ccma.ca

Canadian Education Association

The Canadian Education Association (CEA) serves as a network for leaders in education. The organization examines the latest trends and connects them with innovative ideas and important research focusing not only on Canada, but on the international community as well. Founded in 1891, this bilingual organization works to improve education in Canada.

Services provided to CEA members include publication of a magazine, *Education Canada,* as well as a newsletter and other publications; an annual conference and general meeting; workshops dealing with issues facing Canadian schools; a CEA handbook providing connections with concerned educators throughout Canada; a specialized library containing comprehensive education information from across Canada; and cooperative relationships with other organizations.

For more information contact:

Canadian Education Association
  317 Adelaide Street West, Suite 300
  Toronto, Ontario M5V 1P9

Canadian Library Association

The Canadian Library Association is made up of five constituent divisions, including several that focus on libraries in schools and colleges. These include the following:

1. The Canadian Association of College and University Libraries (CACUL), which includes a Community and Technical College (CTCL) section
2. The Canadian Association of Public Libraries (CAPL), including the Canadian Association of Children's Librarians (CACL) section (600 members)

3. The Canadian Association of Special Libraries and Information Services
4. The Canadian Library Trustees' Association
5. The Canadian School Library Association, which includes the School Library Administrators (SLAS)

The association publishes monographs and other publications, sponsors meetings and other professional development activities, conducts government relations activities, and provides other services.

For more information contact:

Canadian Library Association
200 Elgin Street, Suite 602
Ottawa, Ontario K2P 1L5

College and University Professional Association for Human Resources

For more than fifty years, this association has served human resource administrators at colleges and universities and others interested in the advancement of human resources in higher education. Members include students as well as human resource professionals.

The association promotes the effective management and development of human resources in higher education. It offers a variety of professional development opportunities including annual conventions, workshops, and seminars. The organization also provides books, monographs, periodicals, and other publications.

For more information contact:

College and University Professional Association
for Human Resources
1233 Twentieth Street NW, Suite 301
Washington, DC 20036-1250

International Association of Administrative Professionals

The International Association of Administrative Professionals (IAAP) boasts some 40,000 members and affiliates and 700 chapters in the United States, Canada, and other nations. Members include administrative assistants, executive secretaries, office coordinators, and other administrative support professionals. Although members represent the corporate sector and various nonprofit organizations, many are employed in schools, colleges, and other educational institutions.

Services provided by the IAAP include enhancing the individual and collective value, image, competence, and influence of administrative professionals; providing information, education, and training and setting standards of excellence; offering the Certified Professional Secretary (CPS) rating, covering the subject areas of finance and business law, office systems and administration, and management; sponsoring an annual international convention and education forum; and providing research findings, publications, and other services.

For more information contact:

International Association of Administrative Professionals
   10502 NW Ambassador Drive
   P.O. Box 20404
   Kansas City, MO 64195-0404

International Association of School Librarianship (IASL)

The International Association of School Librarianship provides an international forum for those interested in promoting effective school library media programs in support of the educational process. Members include college faculty teaching programs for school librarians, as well as students enrolled in such programs.

The organization sponsors a variety of activities and sponsors a number of special interest groups.

For more details contact the organization at:

International Association of School Librarianship
  Box 34069
  Seattle, WA 98124-1069

International Society for Technology in Education

Serving educational technology professionals, ISTE is a nonprofit professional organization with a worldwide membership. It promotes the use of information technology to support and improve learning, teaching, and administration in K–12 education and teacher education.

The society supports members as they work to incorporate computers and other advanced technologies into school settings. It also sponsors special projects, publishes journals and other periodicals, and disseminates findings regarding educational technology on an international level.

For more information contact:

International Society for Technology in Education
  480 Charnelton Street
  Eugene, OR 97401-2626

National Association of Elementary School Principals

The National Association of Elementary School Principals focuses on supporting elementary and middle school education. Formed in 1921, it is the largest professional association for principals from kindergarten through eighth grade, serving approximately 28,000 members in the United States, Canada, and elsewhere.

Members include practicing elementary and middle school principals and assistant principals, college and university faculty, related professional educators, and aspiring principals including teachers, students and others interested in becoming principals.

Services include conventions, government relations activities, publications, recognition programs, research, and other activities.

For more information contact:

National Association of Elementary School Principals
    1615 Duke Street
    Alexandria, VA 22314

National Association of Secondary School Principals

The National Association of Secondary School Principals (NASSP) has served educational administrators since 1916. Most members are principals and assistant principals in public, private, and parochial secondary schools. Other members include central office administrators, professors, and retired educators. The organization has more than 46,000 members in the United States, Canada, and other nations.

Among other activities, the organization provides training and professional development opportunities, supports research studies, and sponsors conferences and publications. It also provides legal protection programs, liability insurance, and other services for members.

For more information contact:

National Association of Secondary School Principals
    1904 Association Drive
    Reston, VA 20191

National Middle School Association

The National Middle School Association (NMSA), established in 1973, is an educational association focusing on improving educational experiences of middle school students. It has more than 20,000 members in the United States, Canada, and other countries.

The organization sponsors activities in areas such as curriculum development, professional preparation, the needs of small and rural schools, and urban educational issues. It also sponsors research and publications and holds professional conferences.

For more information contact:

National Middle School Association
  4151 Executive Parkway, Suite 300
  Westerville, OH 43081

National Staff Development Council

The National Staff Development Council is an association that supports staff development and school improvement. Its focus is on high-quality training programs and other appropriate professional development activities such as study groups, action research, and peer coaching, to name a few.

The organization sponsors conferences and workshops, publishes material of interest to educators, and promotes a code of ethics for staff development, among other activities.

More details are available from:

National Staff Development Council
  P.O. Box 240
  Oxford, OH 45056

Society for College and University Planning

Established in 1965, the Society for College and University Planning (SCUP) is an association focused on the promotion, advancement, and application of effective planning in higher education. The society has more than 4,200 members from the following types of organizations: public and private four-year colleges and universities, two-year colleges, college and university systems, governing/coordinating boards, and companies and other related organizations.

SCUP provides a number of services including conferences, professional networking, and publications.

More information is available from:

Society for College and University Planning
311 Maynard Street
Ann Arbor, MI 48104-2211
www.scup.org

CHAPTER 10

GETTING STARTED

Here are some suggestions for getting started with an educational support career.

FINDING JOB VACANCIES

There are a number of approaches to identifying and pursuing jobs in educational support areas. If you're a student nearing completion of a degree program, a good place to start is your school's career services or job placement office.

The most direct strategy is to contact school districts, colleges, or other potential employers directly and request information on job openings and how you might apply for them. Many schools and other organizations now include such information online; start by checking out their site on the World Wide Web. Or call or write the school's or organization's human resources office for information on where job openings are announced.

You also can consult the classified sections of major newspapers and watch for ads placed by educational institutions. Newspapers published in smaller cities typically include only ads for local job openings, while major newspapers such as the *Washington Post* and *New York Times* often list openings on a regional or national basis.

Except for local openings, the best sources of job information in education institutions are publications targeted specifically to educators. One such source is *Education Week,* a national publication providing a wide range of information about education. This includes job listings from school districts and other educational employers around the country.

For those seeking jobs in colleges or universities, a great source of information is the *Chronicle of Higher Education,* a national newspaper published approximately twice monthly. Along with helpful news about trends and events, each issue includes ads for job openings around the United States and often features positions in Canada and in other nations. Each ad normally includes a brief job description, requirements to be considered, and application deadlines.

Other sources of job information include state employment offices, professional associations (often including websites), more general websites on the job search/career development process, and academic departments at colleges and universities offering programs in educational support areas.

DEVELOPING AN APPROPRIATE BACKGROUND

An educational career is different from most others in that virtually everyone has a great deal of firsthand exposure to the field. While in school from kindergarten or first grade on, most of us have plenty of opportunities to see what an educational career involves.

This is less true for educational support areas than it is for teaching, however. Many of these jobs involve special functions of which many students are unaware. As a result, it's a good idea to gather as much information as possible about any career area in which you're interested.

Following are some steps to take in this direction. You might consider some of them while you're still a student or before you make the commitment of actually taking a job in an educational support area.

- Volunteer in an educational support area. Contact a manager in an area in which you're interested (for example, a library director or a director of counseling services) and volunteer to help out in any way that might be needed. As an alternative, pursue a work-study or part-time position with the same goals in mind.
- Complete an internship at a school or college in an educational support area of interest. In working as an intern, you may be assigned low-level, mundane tasks, but working in an educational environment can nevertheless provide a helpful look at what a career in any respective field might be like.
- Complete an interest inventory. Many schools make available to students interest inventories designed to help in making individual career choices. They provide an analytical look at any one person based on information provided in answering questions. Consider taking a test or two of this type and then discuss it with a counselor.
- Enroll in specialized classes related to a specific educational support area. Potentially interested in a given support area, but not sure? To get an idea, take a class or two. Whether this means studying counseling theory or learning the basics of library management or educational technology, a class can provide a great introduction without making a long-term commitment to any educational support area.
- Read more about working in education. Books, newspapers, journals, and other publications also may serve as helpful sources of information. See Appendix A for some suggested further reading.

ENHANCING EMPLOYMENT POTENTIAL

As noted in previous chapters, job openings in educational support areas have widely varying requirements. Some positions require a master's degree or higher. Others demand certification and experience as a teacher. Still others require specific technical capabilities.

On the other hand, many jobs have less stringent requirements. Some, in fact, are designed as entry-level positions and could be a realistic possibility for breaking into the field.

In general, when hiring new staff, employers in an educational setting consider a candidate's educational background (including certifications, if applicable), previous experience, job-related skills, and overall potential.

Ideally, a job candidate will demonstrate strength in all four areas. Of course, younger job applicants could hardly be expected to have attained extensive job experience, but the stronger the combination of these attributes one can develop, the better.

Educational background. While the choice of a major is important, don't overlook the potential offered by individual courses to enhance your background. If you take a course in educational technology, for instance, that might be a good selling point later. The same may be true for a course in counseling, public relations, or library science, to name just a few.

It may be necessary to look at disciplines outside your major to identify such courses. A course in using presentation software, for example, may be found in your college's information technology program. But even if you are majoring in education or another area, perhaps you can take it as an elective course.

Previous experience. Don't overlook the variety of options for gaining work experience. Part-time employment, summer jobs, internships, or volunteer work may provide valuable work experience. This can be useful for listing on resumes or job applications as well as the more fundamental purpose of expanding your knowledge base.

Job-related skills. Obviously it helps to have significant work experience if you want to demonstrate that you hold specific job-related skills. But even if your experience is limited, use other ways to demonstrate job skills.

For example, complete short courses or seminars and keep records of completion. Take certification exams and provide proof that you have passed them. Develop portfolios, lists of skills, or other evidence of skills you have mastered. In your resume, list not just experience, but the specific competencies you have developed. Any evidence of special skills will potentially work to your advantage.

Overall potential. Job potential can be made evident by factors such as success in previous jobs or volunteer roles, good grades, positive recommendations from teachers or professors, communication skills as evidenced in job interviews, previous leadership positions, evidence of organizational skills, and a positive attitude.

Take advantage of any strengths you might have in any of these areas. If you have substantial weaknesses, develop a plan for making improvements. The right combination of education, experience, skills, and potential can prepare you for a successful career in an educational support area.

APPENDIX A

FURTHER READING

Blaxter, Loraine, Christina Hughes and Malcolm Tight. *The Academic Career Handbook.* Bristol, PA: Open University Press, 1998.

Daresh, John C. *Beginning the Principalship: A Practical Guide for New School Leaders.* Conwin Press, 1997.

Eberts, Marjorie and Mary McGowan. *Opportunities in Education Careers.* Lincolnwood, IL: NTC/Contemporary Publishing, 2000.

Edelfelt, Roy. *Careers in Education.* Lincolnwood, IL: NTC/Contemporary Publishing, 1997.

Farr, Michael J. and Laverne Ludden. *Dictionary of Instructional Programs and Careers.* Indianapolis, IN: Jist Works, 2000.

Heiberger, Mary Morris and Julia Miller Vick. *The Academic Job Search Handbook.* Philadelphia: University of Pennsylvania Press, 1996.

McCabe, Edward and Linda McCabe. *How to Succeed in Academics.* San Diego: Academic Press, 2000.

Moffatt, Courtney and Thomas Moffatt. *How to Get a Teaching Job.* Ally and Bacon, 1999.

Moore, Kathryn and Susan Twombly. *Administrative Careers and the Marketplace.* San Francisco: Jossey-Bass, 1990.

United States Department of Labor. *Dictionary of Occupational Titles.* Fourth Edition, 1991.

The Editors of VGM Career Books. *Resumes for Education Careers.* Lincolnwood, IL: NTC/Contemporary Publishing, 1999.

STATE EDUCATION AGENCIES

For information on certification requirements or for other helpful information on elementary and secondary schools in a state in which you'd be interested in working, contact the appropriate state education agency.

This list is provided courtesy of the U.S. Department of Education.

Alabama

Alabama Department of Education
   Gordon Persons Office Building
   50 North Ripley Street
   P.O. Box 302102
   Montgomery, AL 36130-2101
   www.alsde.edu

Alaska

Alaska Department of Education and Early Development
   Suite 200
   801 West Tenth Street
   Juneau, AK 99801-1894
   www.eed.state.ak.us

Arizona

Arizona Department of Education
  1535 West Jefferson
  Phoenix, AZ 85007
  www.ade.state.az.us/

Arkansas

Arkansas Department of Education
  General Education Division
  Room 304 A
  Four State Capitol Mall
  Little Rock, AR 72201-1071
  www.arkedu.state.ar.us/

California

California Department of Education
  Second Floor
  721 Capitol Mall
  Sacramento, CA 94244-2720
  www.cde.ca.gov/

Colorado

Colorado Department of Education
  201 East Colfax Avenue
  Denver, CO 80203-1704
  www.cde.state.co.us/

Connecticut

Connecticut Department of Education
  Room 305
  State Office Building
  165 Capitol Avenue
  Hartford, CT 06106-1080
  www.state.ct.us/sde/

Delaware

Delaware Department of Education
  John G. Townsend Building
  P.O. Box 1402
  Federal and Loockerman Streets
  Dover, DE 19903-1402
  www.doe.state.de.us

District of Columbia

District of Columbia Public Schools
  The Presidential Building
  825 North Capitol Street NE
  Washington, DC 20002
  www.k12.dc.us

Florida

Florida Department of Education
  Room PL 08
  Capitol Building
  Tallahassee, FL 32399-0400
  www.firn.edu/doe/index.html

Georgia

Georgia Department of Education
  2054 Twin Towers East
  205 Butler Street
  Atlanta, GA 30334-5001
  www.doe.k12.ga.us/

Hawaii

Hawaii Department of Education
  1390 Miller Street
  Honolulu, HI 96813
  www.k12.hi.us/

Idaho

Idaho Department of Education
　　Len B. Jordan Office Building
　　650 West State Street
　　P.O. Box 83720
　　Boise, ID 83720-0027
　　www.sde.state.id.us/Dept/

Illinois

Illinois State Board of Education
　　100 North First Street
　　Springfield, IL 62777
　　www.isbe.state.il.us/

Indiana

Indiana Department of Education
　　State House, Room 229
　　Indianapolis, IN 46204-2798
　　www.doe.state.in.us

Iowa

Iowa Department of Education
　　Grimes State Office Building
　　East Fourteenth and Grand Streets
　　Des Moines, IA 50319-0146
　　www.state.ia.us/educate/

Kansas

Kansas Department of Education
　　120 South East Tenth Avenue
　　Topeka, KS 66612-1182
　　www.ksbe.state.ks.us/

Kentucky

Kentucky Department of Education
  1930 Capital Plaza Tower
  500 Mero Street
  Frankfort, KY 40601
  www.kde.state.ky.us/

Louisiana

Louisiana Department of Education
  626 North Fourth Street
  P.O. Box 94064
  Baton Rouge, LA 70704-9064
  www.doe.state.la.us/

Maine

Maine Department of Education
  23 State House Station
  Augusta, ME 04333-0023

Maryland

Maryland Department of Education
  200 West Baltimore Street
  Baltimore, MD 21201
  www.msde.state.md.us

Massachusetts

Massachusetts Department of Education
  Educational Improvement Group
  350 Main Street
  Malden, MA 02148
  www.doe.mass.edu

Michigan

Michigan Department of Education
  Hannah Building
  Fourth Floor
  608 West Allegan Street
  Lansing, MI 48933
  www.mde.state.mi.us/

Minnesota

Minnesota Department of Children, Families, and Learning
  1500 Highway 36 West
  Roseville, MN 55113-4266
  www.cfl.state.mn.us

Mississippi

Mississippi State Department of Education
  Suite 365
  359 North West Street
  Jackson, MS 39201
  www.mde.k12.ms.us/

Missouri

Missouri Department of Elementary and Secondary Education
  P.O. Box 480
  Jefferson City, MO 65102-0480
  www.dese.state.mo.us

Montana

Montana Office of Public Instruction
  P.O. Box 202501
  Helena, MT 59620-2501
  www.metnet.state.mt.us/MAIN.html

Nebraska

Nebraska Department of Education
  301 Centennial Mall South
  P.O. Box 94987
  Lincoln, NE 68509-4987
  www.nde.state.ne.us/

Nevada

Nevada State Department of Education
  700 East Fifth Street
  Carson City, NV 89701
  www.nsn.k12.nv.us/nvdoe/

New Hampshire

New Hampshire Department of Education
  101 Pleasant Street
  State Office Park South
  Concord, NH 03301
  www.state.nh.us/doe/

New Jersey

New Jersey Department of Education
  P.O. Box 500
  100 Riverview
  Trenton, NJ 08625-0500
  www.state.nj.us/education

New Mexico

New Mexico State Department of Education
  Education Building
  300 Don Gaspar
  Santa Fe, NM 87501-2786
  www.sde.state.nm.us/

New York

New York Education Department
   111 Education Building
   Washington Avenue
   Albany, NY 12234
   www.nysed.gov

North Carolina

North Carolina Department of Public Instruction
   Education Building
   301 North Wilmington Street
   Raleigh, NC 27601-2825
   www.dpi.state.nc.us

North Dakota

North Dakota Department of Public Instruction
   11th Floor
   Department 201
   600 East Boulevard Avenue
   Bismarck, ND 58505-0440
   www.dpi.state.nd.us/

Ohio

Ohio Department of Education
   Room 1005
   65 South Front Street
   Columbus, OH 43215-4183
   www.ode.state.oh.us/

Oklahoma

Oklahoma State Department of Education
   2500 North Lincoln Boulevard
   Oklahoma City, OK 73105-4599
   www.sde.state.ok.us

Oregon

Oregon Department of Education
  255 Capitol Street NE
  Salem, OR 97310-0203

Pennsylvania

Pennsylvania Department of Education
  10th Floor
  333 Market Street
  Harrisburg, PA 17126-0333
  www.pde.psu.edu/

Rhode Island

Rhode Island Department of Elementary and Secondary
    Education
  255 Westminster Street
  Providence, RI 02903-3400
  www.ridoe.net/

South Carolina

South Carolina Department of Education
  1006 Rutledge Building
  1429 Senate Street
  Columbia, SC 29201
  www.state.sc.us/sde

South Dakota

South Dakota Department of Education and Cultural Affairs
  700 Governors Drive
  Pierre, SD 57501-2291
  www.state.sd.us/deca/

Tennessee

Tennessee State Department of Education
Andrew Johnson Tower, Sixth Floor
710 James Robertson Parkway
Nashville, TN 37243-0375
www.state.tn.us/education/

Texas

Texas Education Agency
William B. Travis Building
1701 North Congress Avenue
Austin, TX 78701-1494
www.tea.state.tx.us/

Utah

Utah State Office of Education
250 East 500 South
Salt Lake City, UT 84111
www.usoe.k12.ut.us

Vermont

Vermont Department of Education
120 State Street
Montpelier, VT 05620-2501
www.state.vt.us/educ

Virginia

Virginia Department of Education
P.O. Box 2120
101 North Fourteenth Street
Richmond, VA 23218-2120
www.pen.k12.va.us/go/VDOE

Washington

Office of Superintendent of Public Instruction (Washington)
   Old Capitol Building
   600 South Washington
   P.O. Box 47200
   Olympia, WA 98504-7200
   www.k12.wa.us

West Virginia

West Virginia Department of Education
   Building 6
   1900 Kanawha Boulevard East
   Charleston, WV 25305-0330
   www.wvde.state.wv.us

Wisconsin

Wisconsin Department of Public Instruction
   125 South Webster Street
   P.O. Box 7841
   Madison, WI 53707-7841
   www.dpi.state.wi.us

Wyoming

Wyoming Department of Education
   Second Floor
   2300 Capitol Avenue
   Cheyenne, WY 82002
   www.k12.wy.us/wdehome.html

U.S. TERRITORIES

American Samoa

American Samoa Department of Education
   Pago Pago, AS 96799

Commonwealth of the Northern Mariana Islands

Commonwealth of the Northern Mariana Islands Public
    School System
   P.O. Box 1370
   Saipan, MP 96950
   www.saipan.com/gov/branches/pss/index.htm

Guam

Guam Department of Education
   P.O. Box DE
   Agana, GM 96932
   www.doe.edu.gu/

Puerto Rico

Puerto Rico Department of Education
   P.O. Box 190759
   San Juan, PR 00919-0759

Virgin Islands

Virgin Islands Department of Education
   44-46 Kongens Glade
   St. Thomas, VI 00802

STATE HIGHER EDUCATION AGENCIES

For information on financial aid to attend college, contact the state higher education agency in your state. Many of these agencies also provide other information such as contact information for colleges and universities.

This list is provided courtesy of the U.S. Department of Education.

Alabama

Alabama Commission on Higher Education
P.O. Box 302000
Montgomery, AL 36130-2000
www.ache.state.al.us/

Alaska

Alaska Commission on Postsecondary Education
3030 Vintage Boulevard
Juneau, AK 99801-7109
www.state.ak.us/acpe/home.html

Arizona

Arizona Commission for Postsecondary Education
   Suite 275
   2020 North Central Avenue
   Phoenix, AZ 85004-4503
   www.acpe.asu.edu/

Arkansas

Arkansas Department of Higher Education
   114 East Capitol
   Little Rock, AR 72201-3818
   www.adhe.arknet.edu/

California

California Student Aid Commission
   P.O. Box 416026
   Rancho Cordova, CA 95741-9026
   www.csac.ca.gov/

Colorado

Colorado Commission on Higher Education
   Colorado History Museum, Second Floor
   1300 Broadway
   Denver, CO 80203
   www.state.co.us/cche_dir/hecche.html

Connecticut

Connecticut Department of Higher Education
   61 Woodland Street
   Hartford, CT 06105-2391
   www.ctdhe.commnet.edu/

Delaware

Delaware Higher Education Commission
    Carvel State Office Building
    820 North French Street
    Wilmington, DE 19801
    www.doe.state.de.us/high-ed/

District of Columbia

District of Columbia Department of Human Services
    Office of Postsecondary Education, Research, and Assistance
    Suite 401
    2100 Martin Luther King, Jr. Avenue SE
    Washington, DC 20020
    www.dhs.washington.dc.us/

Florida

Florida Board of Regents
    325 West Gaines Street
    Florida Education Center
    Tallahassee, FL 32339

Georgia

Georgia Student Finance Authority
    State Loans and Grants Division
    Suite 200
    2082 East Exchange Place
    Tucker, GA 30084
    www.gsfc.org

Hawaii

Hawaii State Postsecondary Education Commission
    Room 209, 2444 Dole Street
    Honolulu, HI 96822-2302
    www.hern.hawaii.edu/hern/

Idaho

Idaho State Board of Education
    P.O. Box 83720
    Boise, ID 83720-0027
    www.sde.state.id.us/Dept/

Illinois

Illinois Student Assistance Commission
    1755 Lake Cook Road
    Deerfield, IL 60015-5209
    www.isac-online.org/

Indiana

State Student Assistance Commission of Indiana
    Suite 500
    150 West Market Street
    Indianapolis, IN 46204-2811

Iowa

Iowa College Student Aid Commission
    Fourth Floor
    200 Tenth Street
    Des Moines, IA 50309
    www.state.ia.us/collegeaid/

Kansas

Kansas Board of Regents
    Suite 1410
    700 SW Harrison
    Topeka, KS 66603-3760
    www.kansasregents.org/

Kentucky

Kentucky Higher Education Assistance Authority
  1050 U.S. Highway 127 South
  Frankfort, KY 40601-4323
  www.kheaa.com

Louisiana

Louisiana Office of Student Financial Assistance
  P.O. Box 91202
  Baton Rouge, LA 70821-9202
  www.osfa.state.la.us/

Maine

Maine Education Assistance Division
  Finance Authority of Maine (FAME)
  5 Community Drive
  Augusta, ME 04332-0949
  www.famemaine.com/

Maryland

Maryland Higher Education Commission
  Jeffrey Building
  16 Francis Street
  Annapolis, MD 21401-1781
  www.mhec.state.md.us/

Massachusetts

Massachusetts Board of Higher Education
  Room 1401
  One Ashburton Place
  Boston, MA 02108
  www.mass.edu/

Massachusetts Higher Education Information Center
  Boston Public Library
  700 Boylston Street
  Boston, MA 02116
  www.heic.org/

Michigan

Michigan Higher Education Assistance Authority
  Office of Scholarships and Grants
  P.O. Box 30462
  Lansing, MI 48909-7962
  www.MI-StudentAid.org/

Minnesota

Minnesota Higher Education Services Office
  Suite 350
  1450 Energy Park Drive
  Saint Paul, MN 55108-5227
  www.mheso.state.mn.us/

Mississippi

Mississippi Postsecondary Education Financial Assistance Board
  3825 Ridgewood Road
  Jackson, MS 39211-6453
  www.ihl.state.ms.us

Missouri

Missouri Department of Higher Education
  3515 Amazonas Drive
  Jefferson City, MO 65109-5717
  www.mocbhe.gov/

Montana

Montana University System
  2500 Broadway
  P.O. Box 203101
  Helena, MT 59620-3103
  www.montana.edu/wwwoche

Nebraska

Nebraska Coordinating Commission for Postsecondary Education
  P.O. Box 95005
  Lincoln, NE 68509-5005
  www.nol.org/NEpostsecondaryed/

New Hampshire

New Hampshire Postsecondary Education Commission
  2 Industrial Park Drive
  Concord, NH 03301-8512
  www.state.nh.us/postsecondary/

New Jersey

New Jersey Higher Education Student Assistance Authority
  Building 4
  P.O. Box 540
  Quakerbridge Plaza
  Trenton, NJ 08625-0540
  www.state.nj.us/treasury/osa

New Mexico

New Mexico Commission on Higher Education
  1068 Cerrillos Road
  Santa Fe, NM 87501
  www.nmche.org/

New York

New York State Higher Education Services Corporation
  99 Washington Avenue
  Albany, NY 12255
  www.hesc.com

North Carolina

North Carolina State Education Assistance Authority
  P.O. Box 13663
  Research Triangle Park, NC 27709-3663
  www.ncseaa.edu/

North Dakota

North Dakota University System
  North Dakota Student Financial Assistance Program
  Department 215
  600 East Boulevard Avenue
  Bismarck, ND 58505-0230
  www.nodak.edu/

Ohio

Ohio Board of Regents
  State Grants and Scholarships Department
  P.O. Box 182452
  Columbus, OH 43218-2452
  www.regents.state.oh.us/sgs/

Oklahoma

Oklahoma State Regents for Higher Education
  Oklahoma Guaranteed Student Loan Program
  P.O. Box 3000
  Oklahoma City, OK 73101-3000
  www.okhighered.org/

Oregon

Oregon Student Assistance Commission
Suite 100
1500 Valley River Drive
Eugene, OR 97401
www.ossc.state.or.us

Oregon University System
P.O. Box 3175
Eugene, OR 97401
www.ous.edu/

Pennsylvania

Pennsylvania Higher Education Assistance Agency
1200 North Seventh Street
Harrisburg, PA 17102-1444
www.pheaa.org

Rhode Island

Rhode Island Higher Education Assistance Authority
560 Jefferson Boulevard
Warwick, RI 02886
www.riheaa.org

Rhode Island Office of Higher Education
301 Promenade Street
Providence, RI 02908-5748
www.uri.edu/ribog/riohe.htm

South Carolina

South Carolina Higher Education Tuition Grants Commission
Suite 811
1310 Lady Street
P.O. Box 12159
Columbia, SC 29201
www.state.sc.us/tuitiongrants

South Dakota

South Dakota Board of Regents
    Suite 200
    306 East Capitol Avenue
    Pierre, SD 57501
    www.ris.sdbor.edu/

Tennessee

Tennessee Higher Education Commission
    Parkway Towers, Suite 1900
    404 James Robertson Parkway
    Nashville, TN 37243-0830
    www.state.tn.us/thec/index.htm

Texas

Texas Higher Education Coordinating Board
    P.O. Box 12788
    Austin, TX 78711
    www.thecb.state.tx.us

Utah

Utah State Board of Regents
    Three Triad Center, Suite 550
    355 West North Temple
    Salt Lake City, UT 84180-1205
    www.utahsbr.edu/

Vermont

Vermont Student Assistance Corporation
    Champlain Mill
    1 Main Street, Fourth Floor
    P.O. Box 2000
    Winooski, VT 05404-2601
    www.vsac.org/

Virginia

State Council of Higher Education for Virginia
  James Monroe Building, Ninth Floor
  101 North Fourteenth Street
  Richmond, VA 23219
  www.schev.edu/

Washington

Washington State Higher Education Coordinating Board
  P.O. Box 43430
  917 Lakeridge Way
  Olympia, WA 98504-3430
  www.hecb.wa.gov

West Virginia

State College and University Systems of West Virginia
  1018 Kanawha Boulevard, East
  Charleston, WV 25301
  www.scusco.wvnet.edu

Wisconsin

Wisconsin Higher Educational Aids Board
  131 West Wilson Street
  Madison, WI 53707-7885
  www.heab.state.wi.us

Wyoming

Wyoming Community College Commission
  Eighth Floor
  2020 Carey Avenue
  Cheyenne, WY 82002
  www.commission.wcc.edu/

CANADIAN DEPARTMENTS AND MINISTRIES OF EDUCATION

Following is contact information for departments and ministries responsible for education in Canada's provinces and territories. This list is taken from the Council of Ministers of Education and can be found at www.cmec.ca/educmin.stm.

Alberta

Department of Learning
    West Tower, Devonian Building
    11160 Jasper Avenue
    Edmonton, AB
    T5K 0L2
    www.learning.gov.ab.ca/

British Columbia

Ministry of Education
    P.O. Box 9156, Stn. Prov. Govt.
    Victoria, BC
    V8W 9H2
    www.bced.gov.bc.ca/

Ministry of Advanced Education, Training and Technology
  P.O. Box 9884, Stn. Prov. Govt.
  Victoria, BC
  V8W 9T6
  www.aett.gov.bc.ca/

Manitoba

Department of Education and Training
  Legislative Building
  450 Broadway
  Winnipeg, MB
  R3C 0V8
  www.gov.mb.ca/educate/

New Brunswick

Department of Education
  P.O. Box 6000
  Fredericton, NB
  E3B 5H1
  www.gov.nb.ca/education

Department of Training and Employment Development
  P.O. Box 6000
  Fredericton, NB
  E3B 5H1
  www.gov.nb.ca/dol-mdt

Newfoundland and Labrador

Department of Education
  3rd Floor, Confederation Building, West Block
  Box 8700
  St. John's, NF
  A1B 4J6
  www.gov.nf.ca/edu/

Northwest Territories

Department of Education, Culture and Employment
  P.O.Box 1320
  4501-50 Avenue
  Yellowknife, NT
  X1A 2L9
  www.siksik.learnnet.nt.ca

Nova Scotia

Department of Education
  Box 578
  Halifax, NS
  B3J 2S9
  www.ednet.ns.ca/

Nunavut

Department of Education
  P.O. Box 800
  Government of Nunavut
  Building 1088E
  Iqaluit, Nunavut
  X0A 0H0
  www.nunavut.com/education/english/index.html

Ontario

Ministry of Education
  Mowat Block
  900 Bay Street
  Toronto, ON
  M7A 1L2
  www.edu.gov.on.ca/

Prince Edward Island

Department of Education
  Box 2000
  Sullivan Building, 2nd and 3rd Floors, 16 Fitzroy St.
  Charlottetown, PE
  C1A 7N8
  www.gov.pe.ca/education

Québec

Ministère de L'Éducation
  Édifice Marie-Guyart
  28e étage, 1035, rue de la Chevrotière
  Québec, QC
  G1R 5A5
  www.meg.gouv.qc.ca/

Saskatchewan

Department of Education
  2220 College Avenue
  Regina, SK
  S4P 3V7
  www.sasked.gov.sk.ca/

Yukon

Department of Education
  P.O Box 2703
  Whitehorse, YK
  Y1A 2C6
  www.gov.yk.ca/depts/education/